Hermit Crabs
FOR
DUMMIES®

by Kelli A. Wilkins

WILEY

Wiley Publishing, Inc.

Hermit Crabs For Dummies®

Published by
Wiley Publishing, Inc.
111 River St.
Hoboken, NJ 07030-5774
www.wiley.com

Publisher's Acknowledgements

Project Editor: Laura B. Peterson
Acquisitions Editor: Stacy Kennedy
Technical Editor: Christa Wilkin
Composition Services: Indianapolis Composition Services Department
Cover Photo: © Dorling Kindersky/Getty Images
Cartoon: Rich Tennant, www.the5thwave.com

About the Author

Kelli A. Wilkins is a freelance writer experienced in keeping and rescuing a variety of pets. She graduated from Hofstra University with a degree in Communications and recently completed the Commercial Writer's program at Middlesex County College. The former Assistant Editor of *Reptile & Amphibian Hobbyist* magazine, Kelli lives in New Jersey.

This book is dedicated to the whole Kelly clan and to Robert for supporting me every step of the way.

Author's Acknowledgments

I want to thank my Acquisitions Editor, Stacy Kennedy; my Project Editor, Laura Peterson; and my Technical Editor, Christa Wilkin, president of the Hermit Crab Association (www.hermitcrabassociation.com), for all her experience and help.

Table of Contents

The 5th Wave
By Rich Tennant

"Hermit crabs are arthropods! I wish you'd quit referring to them as members of the hors d'oeuvres family."

Chapter 1

Choosing Crustaceans: All About Hermit Crabs

In This Chapter

▶ Using this book effectively

▶ Defining a hermit crab

▶ Understanding the different types of crabs

▶ Checking out hermit crab anatomy

*W*elcome to the world of hermit crabs! Although they are unusual pets, hermit crabs (or *hermies*, as their keepers affectionately call them) are very popular with people of all ages. Maybe you're a parent buying this book for your child or a kid buying it with your hard-earned cash. Maybe you just bought a hermit crab and need the essential scoop on getting set up as well as some general care info, or you've had one for a while but want a refresher on the best way to care for your hermie. No matter what your reason, this book gives you all the information you need to choose the right crab and take care of its every need, without bogging you down in lots of technical stuff. Although several hundred types of hermit crabs live around the world (including marine hermit crabs), this book focuses on six land hermit crabs that are commonly kept as pets in the United States.

First Things First: Using This Book

Hermit Crabs For Dummies is designed so you can find the answer to a specific question easily, without reading through lots of information you don't want at that particular moment. Begin with Chapter 4 if you need basic setup information, flip to Chapter 5 if you need to know what to do with a molting crab, or head to Chapter 2 if you're still on the fence about adding hermit crabs to your family. Or if you prefer, start at the beginning and read until you hit the back cover.

As you read, keep an eye out for text in *italics*, which indicates a new term and a nearby definition — so there's no need to spend time hunting through a glossary. The `monofont` points out Web addresses worth checking out for additional information. You also run into a few sidebars (the occasional gray box); although the information in the sidebars is good, it's not essential to the discussion at hand, so skip 'em if you want to.

Be on the lookout for the following icons sprinkled throughout the text that point out important information:

This symbol draws attention to dangerous situations or common mistakes hermit crab owners can make.

This icon points out helpful hints or tips that make your life (and hermit crab keeping) easier.

You see this icon whenever there is crucial information to keep in mind.

This icon highlights technical information. If you're in a hurry, you can skip this material and come back to it later.

This icon highlights hermit crab care or behavior unique to a certain type or species of hermit crab.

You can find any other information you need in either the table of contents or the index. Have fun with your hermits!

What Is a Hermit Crab Anyway?

So just what is a hermit crab? You may be surprised to learn that the term *hermit crab* is a misnomer. Hermit crabs aren't hermits, and they aren't crabs either (at least not in the true sense).

Thoroughly confused? Not a problem. This section sorts the mystery out by taking a look at both true crabs and hermit crabs.

True or false? Hermit crabs are not crabs

True crabs, like the one in Figure 1-1, are commonly found along seashores and are related to lobsters and shrimp. They have five pairs of legs (four of which are used for walking) and a hard shell that protects their short abdomens.

Photo credit: PhotoDisc, Inc.

Figure 1-1: True crabs have hard shells covering their entire bodies.

Although hermit crabs have many features similar to true crabs (they both live by the seashore and have five pairs of legs, for example), they look quite different, as you can tell from Figure 1-2. Here is a short list of some differences between the two:

- ✔ Hermit crabs have long abdomens that curl under their bodies.

- ✔ Hermit crabs have no protective shell on their abdomen (like true crabs do), so they live in "borrowed" snail shells.

- ✔ Hermit crabs use only three pairs of legs for walking.

- ✔ Hermit crabs have longer antennae.

Photo credit: IHaveCrabs.com/Andrew Lewis

Figure 1-2: Hermit crabs spend their lives in borrowed snail shells.

Hardly hermits: The life of a hermit crab

Hermit crabs are actually quite sociable creatures. In the wild, they live in colonies and often travel in packs of up to 100 crabs. They got the misleading "hermit" label by carrying their homes around on their backs and retreating into their shells when they sense danger.

Hermit crabs are *nocturnal* (which means they are most active at night), so during the day they conceal themselves from the harsh sun (and predators) by hiding out under trees, driftwood, leaves, and rocks or by burying themselves in the sand. But during the cooler evening hours, they wander the beach looking for food, searching for new shells, and mating. They are quite adventurous and have been known to travel a mile or two from the ocean.

Hermit crabs are scavengers, and they eat whatever they find. They like meat, fruits, and vegetables, and they also enjoy munching on bark and decaying driftwood they find along the seashore.

Although not picky about their diet, hermit crabs are very particular about their shells (actually snail shells), which offer them much-needed protection in the wild. The crabs always seem to be on the lookout for a newer, bigger, or better shell to move in to (it's keeping up with the Joneses, hermit crab style).

If you find a hermit crab in the wild, don't disturb it or collect it for a pet. It could be a female crab making her way to the ocean to lay eggs and continue the life cycle of these creatures. Hermit crabs collected in this way usually die quickly because of the stress of being removed from the wild. In some areas, it's illegal to collect wild hermit crabs.

Pick Me, Pick Me! Exploring the Six Types of Land Hermit Crabs

Although there are hundreds of types of hermit crabs in the wild around the world, only six are commonly kept as pets in the United States. Many hermit crab hobbyists use the technical or scientific names when discussing the different hermit crabs, which are all in the genus *Coenobita*. However, most of these hermit crabs also have plain English (or common) names, so you don't have to worry about understanding Latin to read about your pets. I give you both the common and the scientific names, however. (If you want to know where the technical names come from, check out the sidebar "Where does hermie get his scientific name?")

Where does hermie get his scientific name?

Scientists have divided all living things into different classifications, each with a specific scientific (or *taxonomic*) name. Without delving into too much technical detail, here's what you need to know to understand the scientific naming of hermit crabs.

The most general classification is the *Kingdom Animalia*, which contains all the animals on Earth. Hermit crabs belong to one of the largest groups of animals — the arthropods (known as *Phylum Arthropoda*). Simply put, arthropods are invertebrates that have jointed legs and a hard outer covering called an *exoskeleton*.

The *Phylum Arthropoda* is further broken down and includes the *Class Crustacea*. (This is where we get the name crustacean, which refers to crabs.) The crustaceans are divided into Orders. Crabs, lobsters, and shrimp are all in the *Order Decapoda* (which means ten-legged).

The decapods are divided into specific Families. Hermit crabs are members of the *Family Coenobitidae*. This Family is divided down once again, and our pet hermit crabs are grouped in the *Genus Coenobita*. Although there are many different species of hermit crabs, the six found in the U.S. hobby are called *clypeatus, compressus, brevimanus, rugosus, cavipes,* and *perlatus*. Now wasn't that easy?

The *purple pincher* or *Caribbean crabs* (*Coenobita clypeatus*) are the most common (see the purple pincher crab back in Figure 1-2). You can find them in red, brown, and purple color variations. Their left front claw is larger than the right and is usually purple (thus the name purple pincher crab), and their eyes are round. These crabs are found throughout the Caribbean, the Florida Keys, the Virgin Islands, Venezuela, and the West Indies.

The *Ecuadorian hermit crabs* or *E-crabs* (*Coenobita compressus*) are the second most common hermie pet. They are varying shades of tan, gray, yellow, and orange. Sometimes their walking legs are a darker shade than the rest of their body. They have striping on the sides of their heads, teardrop-shaped eyes, a large left claw, and a wide, flat body. (See the E-crab in Figure 1-3.) Overall, they are more active than their purple pincher cousins and run a lot faster. Ecuadorians live on the Pacific coast from Baja California south to Argentina.

The other four types of hermit crabs are less common but are growing in popularity:

- ✔ The *Indonesian purple hermit crab (Coenobita brevimanus)* is the largest hermit crab of the species and is usually lilac purple or brown in color. It's often considered the most relaxed of the hermit crabs. It hails from the Pacific rim.

- ✔ *Coenobita cavipes* doesn't have a common name and usually just goes by "cavipes." This shy crab has red antennae and a black, bluish, or red body. It is found off the east coast of Africa and in Indonesian and West Pacific areas.

- ✔ *Coenobita rugosus* doesn't have a common name either, but is affectionately called "rugs" or ruggies." It's also known as the "crying" hermit crab because of the strange sounds that it makes when it's upset. It comes in all the colors of the rainbow — chocolate, peach, white, blue, brown, tan, and even bright red — and is native to the West Pacific and Indonesian areas.

- ✔ The *strawberry* or *red hermit crab* (*Coenobita perlatus*) is the rarest of the six. It's a bright red-orange with white bumps all over the legs and claws, which makes it look like a strawberry (hence the name). It has very unique eyes that look like polished hematite. Its native range is from the Red Sea to the West Pacific.

Unfortunately, if you go to a pet store and ask for one of these hermit crabs specifically, you may have some difficulty. Most pet store employees, while they'll do their best to help you out, probably aren't hermit crab experts and may not be able to tell you which species they sell.

Photo credit: IHave Crabs.com/Andrew Lewis

Figure 1-3: Caribbean hermit crabs have round eyes and large left claws.

But not to worry — you can take care of all six types the same way (with a few minor exceptions that I'll tell you about), and they all make great pets, so you can just pick out the cutest one in the tank. (Check out Chapter 3 for info on how to pick out a healthy hermie that's right for you.) However, if you want to identify the hermie you just brought home or to take a guess at what kinds are in your local pet store, check out the following Web sites for some great color photos and identifying tips:

- ✔ www.mrspoppypuff.com/species.htm
- ✔ www.hermit-crabs.com/exotics.html
- ✔ www.ihavecrabs.com/crabidentifier.php

What's Under That Shell? The Anatomy of a Hermit Crab

If you are going to keep hermit crabs as pets, familiarizing yourself with their basic anatomy is a good idea. I go through the individual body parts of the crab in plain English in the following sections. The diagram in Figure 1-4 gives you a rough idea of where everything goes.

So now, without further ado, let's take a peek under that shell.

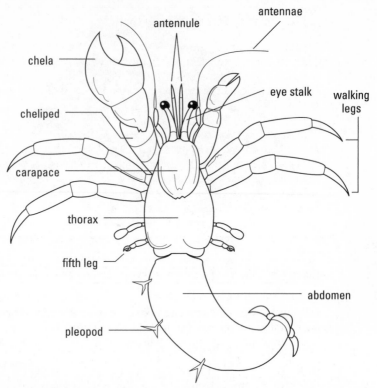

chela

cheliped

carapace

thorax

fifth leg

pleopod

antennule

antennae

eye stalk

walking legs

abdomen

Figure 1-4: You can use this diagram of little hermie's anatomy as a reference.

The body and exoskeleton

Hermit crabs are divided into three sections: the head, the *thorax* (main body section), and the abdomen. The hermit crab's body, including its legs and claws, is covered by an *exoskeleton,* a hard, protective covering made of *chitin,* which is primarily calcium. Over the head and back, the exoskeleton forms an especially hard shield called a *carapace.* To grow, a hermit crab has to shed its exoskeleton in a process known as *molting.* (For a detailed discussion on molting and how to care for your hermie during this process, refer to Chapter 5.) A new exoskeleton is constantly being formed underneath the old one. The abdomen, however, is soft and vulnerable, which is why hermits must find other shells to live in. Snail shells are a natural choice for hermie's protective home because they naturally curve to the right, as does hermie's abdomen.

The legs and claws

Hermit crabs are *decapods*, which means they have ten legs (or five pairs of legs). But if you take a look at your average hermit crab, you don't see all ten legs. In fact, the only time you can see all five pairs of legs on a hermit crab is when he (or she) decides to leave the shell.

The first thing you notice about the first pair of legs (called *chelipeds*) are the claws, called *chela*. The left claw is larger than the right, and the crab uses it for climbing and defense. When threatened or to conserve moisture in the shell, your hermie can close off the entrance to his shell with this claw. The smaller right claw is used for climbing and eating.

All about breeding

Hermit crabs can't reproduce in captivity as they do in the wild. Scientists (with some degree of success) have attempted the process, but overall, it's too complicated for the average hobbyist to consider.

When mating, the hermit crabs extend about ¾ of the way out of their shells. The male uses his flexible fifth pair of legs to place his *spermatophore* into the female's *gonopore*. (These are genital openings located on the first segment of the female's back pair of walking legs.)

After the crabs have mated, the female attaches the eggs to her abdomen inside her shell and carries them around with her until they are ready to hatch. Female hermit crabs can produce thousands of eggs at one time. This is necessary because many of the young crabs don't survive into adulthood.

Hermit crab eggs must be hatched in salt water in order to survive, so when the female crab is ready to release her eggs, she wanders down to the seashore. She uses the tiny pinchers on the end of her fifth pair of legs to snip each cluster of eggs from her body. Then she passes the eggs up her body to her mouthparts, which deposit the eggs onto her pinchers. The crab then quickly flicks the eggs into the ocean. The eggs hatch upon contact with sea water and the little creatures (I'll call them "baby" hermit crabs for now) are released.

"Baby" hermit crabs go through several stages of development before they resemble adult hermit crabs. They swim around in the ocean and feed on small animals. Each little hermit crab goes through several molts (usually three or four) and eventually makes its way to the beach to search for snail shells to call home.

The second and third pairs of legs are called *ambulatory* or walking legs. The fourth and fifth sets of legs (*periopods*) are tucked in the crab's shell. The crab uses these smaller legs to hold himself inside the shell (otherwise he would fall out when he was picked up) and maneuver it as he walks around. The fifth set of legs are very flexible and end in tiny pinchers. Hermie uses these to clean the inside of the shell, groom his abdomen, push feces from the shell, and for reproductive purposes.

The gills and mouth

Although hermit crabs can leave the water's edge and travel miles from the sea, they must keep their gills moist. In fact, the crabs store a small supply of water in their shells just to keep their gills wet. Unlike fish, hermits don't submerge their gills in water to breathe. They can drown if they are trapped in water and can't get out. The gills are quite small and are located above the crab's legs on the sides of the thorax.

Hermit crabs also have three small pairs of feeding appendages around and in their mouth (called *maxillipeds*) that help them hold onto food while they nibble away at it. Hermits also use these appendages to groom themselves.

The sensory organs

Hermit crabs' eyes, which are made up of many lenses, are located on the ends of long eyestalks with a joint at the base. (When the crab retreats into his shell, he tucks his eyestalks down between his two claws so they are completely safe.)

Hermit crabs have two pairs of *antennae*, or feelers, on their heads. The longer pair (*antennae*) are located below the eyestalks to the outside and are very sensitive to touch. The hermit crab uses the long antennae to feel its way around and to touch things it comes in contact with (almost like a cat uses its whiskers). The shorter pair (*antennules*) are located between the crab's eyes and are sensitive to odors and aid the crab in finding food. The crab's first pair of ambulatory legs are also sensitive and serve as back-up antennae if needed.

Setae are bristle-like projections on the walking legs that act like touch receptors and allow the hermit crabs to locate food, water, and other crabs. The longer bristles bend when they come into contact with hard surfaces (like rocks, trees, and other objects), while the shorter bristles are sensitive to water currents.

Chapter 2

Is a Hermit Crab Your Perfect Pet?

So you're thinking about joining the hermit crab-owning population. Congratulations! What first attracted you to keeping hermits as pets? Do you have a friend or relative who introduced you to these little guys? Perhaps you saw a tank of hermit crabs for sale in a pet store and wanted a few for yourself.

Whatever first sparked your interest, you're now thinking about bringing a few home. But before you make the actual investment in your new pals, you need to make sure that hermit crabs are the right pet for you.

This chapter outlines the advantages as well as the basic requirements and costs of keeping hermit crabs so that you can make an informed decision. Hopefully, by the time you have all the facts, you'll be ready, willing, and eager to bring some hermies home!

Why Keep Hermit Crabs?

Hermit crabs aren't for everyone. Some people prefer to cuddle up next to a purring cat or like to take long walks with their faithful canine companion. That's fine. But others, for one reason or another (allergies, cost, or space considerations), just can't have a traditional pet. For these people, hermit crabs may be the perfect answer to their unfulfilled pet longings.

Some of the many advantages to owning hermit crabs are:

- Hermit crabs are quiet pets that don't take up a lot of space in your home. Therefore, they are a good choice for people who live in apartments and can't keep cats or dogs.

- Many people are allergic to animal hair or fur. Unlike cats, dogs, rabbits, and other small mammals, hermit crabs don't aggravate anyone's allergies. (And they don't shed — at least not their hair!)

- Hermit crabs are clean, odorless, and easy to take care of. You don't have to scoop out a litter box every day or take your hermit crab for a walk so he can tend to his bathroom needs.

- After you purchase the initial supplies, keeping hermit crabs is pretty inexpensive. They don't need annual veterinary check-ups, medications, or licenses.

- Hermit crabs are happy living in a glass tank (called a *crabitat* by hermie hobbyists) and won't outgrow them quickly as they age (like fish or reptiles can).

Keep in mind, however, that even though hermit crabs are low maintenance, they still have specific needs that must be met if they are to thrive in your home. Hermit crabs aren't temporary or throw-away pets. They are living creatures that deserve appropriate care.

Do some first-hand research on hermit crabs before you decide to purchase them. Seek out other hermit crab enthusiasts and find out what they like most about their pets. How long have they been keeping hermit crabs? Do they have any pet peeves? Some of the sites listed in the "Ten Hermit Crab-Friendly Web Sites" at the back of the book have chatrooms where you can talk to other hermit crab owners.

Got What It Takes? Caring for a Hermit Crab

Before you rush out and bring home a tank filled with hermit crabs, make sure you know how much of your space, time, and money they require. Your hermits will rely on you to provide for all their needs for the rest of their lives which, with proper care, can be more than a decade long. Hermit crabs, like any other pet, need to feel secure in their environment. This means that you have to make them feel at home in your home.

Any vacancies? Finding space for hermits

Hermit crabs come from a warm, moist environment and you need to provide them with the same kind of living conditions in your house. Now don't panic — or get too excited — you don't have to turn your house into a sauna. Just make sure you have the space and resources to create a good crabitat. (For more information on setting up a crabitat, see Chapter 4.)

Finding space for a tank

Before you purchase any hermit crabs, decide how much space you have available to devote to the crabitat. The amount of room you have for a tank determines how many crabs you can bring home. For example, if you only have a small area available in the corner of the living room, you have to get a smaller tank, and thus, fewer crabs.

Keep in mind that hermit crabs are social creatures and need to be kept with other hermies. A single crab will become stressed and possibly ill, even if you play with him every day. So make sure that you have enough space for at least two or three crabs.

Most hermit crab keepers start out with a 10-gallon glass aquarium, which is usually 20 inches long, 10 inches wide, and 12 inches tall. While there is no rule for how many crabs can fit in a 10-gallon tank, allow for about one and a half gallons of space per 1 inch crab. (Measure the crab across the opening of his shell to estimate his size.) You can comfortably house six 1-inch crabs or three 2-inch crabs in a 10-gallon tank. If you are keeping jumbo crabs, you need to invest in a 20-gallon tank, which gives each crab plenty of space to roam around and still leaves room for the crabitat accessories. Remember, the bigger the crabs you have, the larger the tank you need.

If you're new to the hobby or you're buying hermit crabs for a child, stick with two or three crabs and see how you like them. If later on you decide that hermit crab keeping is definitely right for you, add more crabs to the crabitat.

You also need space to store all the pet supplies and tank equipment. A small, sturdy cabinet that can serve as the tank stand as well as storage for supplies is very convenient. That way, you don't have to trek up two flights of stairs to the upstairs closet when it's time to feed the crabs.

Selecting a good crabitat location

You want to set up the crabitat away from drafty doors or windows, direct sunlight, heating ducts, and air conditioning vents. (You don't want your tropical hermit crabs to get a chill!) A corner of the living room or a bedroom is often a good place. (I discuss tank placement in more detail in Chapter 4.)

If you decide to set up the hermit crab tank in your bedroom, keep in mind that these little guys are nocturnal. They like to eat, play, and socialize with other hermies and may keep you awake. If you are a light sleeper, you may want to keep the tank in another room.

Have you got the time?

Although hermies are low maintenance when compared to other animals, you still need to take care of them every day. They can't add water to their own dish or feed themselves if their food bowl is empty.

Here are some of the daily duties of owning a hermie:

- ✔ Check your hermit crabs' food and water dishes and resupply as needed.
- ✔ Mist your hermies with warm water.
- ✔ Check the temperature and humidity levels and make adjustments.
- ✔ Play with your hermit crabs and check for signs of stress.

These tasks take about 15 minutes each day. Ask yourself whether you have that time to devote to your pet. You may want to create a schedule and set aside a specific time every day to tend to your hermit crabs. They will look forward to your visit — especially when they know it's feeding time!

With the proper care, hermit crabs can live 10 years or more. (Some hermit crabs have lived in captivity for 30 years!) Do you have the dedication necessary to care for your hermies for the rest of their lives? If you're unsure, you may want to reconsider hermit crab ownership.

Money, money, money

Hermit crabs are among the least expensive pets to own. Unlike cats and dogs, they never need to be vaccinated, spayed, or neutered or take obedience lessons. And they even like to eat some of the same foods that you do. (That saves a bit on your food bill!) Although keeping hermit crabs won't break your bank account, you do need to be aware of the start-up costs involved.

You can purchase all the necessary equipment to set up your hermit crab tank at your local pet supply shop. Pricing differs from store to store and from location to location around the country, but Table 2-1 gives you an overall idea of the costs involved.

If you're a first time hermit crab owner, you may want to start out small — both in your setup and in your crabs! Don't go overboard and buy a 20-gallon tank and load it up with hermies. Remember that the more crabs you own, the higher your expenses will be.

Table 2-1	Hermit Crab Setup Costs
Item	*Cost (in range)*
10-gallon tank with glass lid	$25
Undertank heater	$16–$20
Hygrometer (often sold with thermometer)	$6
Thermometer	$2–$7
Substrate (sand)	$6 (for a 2-pound bag)
Food and water dishes	$2–$15
Hermit crab food	$2–$7
Isolation tank (for molting or sick crabs)	$14
Sea sponges	$2 each
Sea salt	$8 (for a 10-gallon box)
Stress Coat water conditioner	$2–$6
Hideboxes	$3–$15 each
Toys	$3–$15 each
Extra snail shells (3)	$1–$6 each
Hermit crabs (3)	$5 and up (depending on size)
Total:	**$108–$173**

Some pet supply stores offer hermit crab starter kits that include food, a sea sponge, a few shells, a food or water dish, and a small plastic tank. These kits are designed for small crabs and can be bought for about 20 to 40 dollars. Although they may look like ideal or easy setups, these plastic tanks don't make good crabitats. They are too small to properly house hermit crabs and their vented lids don't retain enough heat and humidity to keep the hermit crabs in good health. Check out Chapter 4 for the best way to house your hermits.

Many hermit crab owners purchase their pet supplies via the Internet from companies that specialize in hermit crab products. A few good suppliers are www.petco.com, www.petdiscounters.com, and www.thehermiehut.com. Do some research and see whether this is a good option for you and your budget.

Although the start-up costs may seem a bit overwhelming when you first look at them, after you buy everything you need for the tank, your only costs are for substrate, food, and shells. This should average less than $10 a month, depending on how much fresh fruits and vegetables you buy for your hermits.

Quality counts, so buy the best setup your budget allows. Shop around if you have to. Don't skimp on the essential items like the tank, hygrometer, thermometer, and heater; your crabs need these items most to stay alive and healthy.

Make certain that you really want to keep hermits before you invest in them. Don't buy them because a friend has some and wants you to own them, too. Avoid buying on impulse just because you saw them for sale in the mall or on the boardwalk. (Besides, those are really bad places to buy hermit crabs — see Chapter 3 for important tips on buying hermies.) Think the situation over carefully so that everyone (including the crabs!) is happy.

Is your house a good atmosphere for hermie?

Let's face it, some homes are pet-friendly and some aren't. Hermies need to be kept in a warm and humid, and they really don't like to be poked and prodded all day (especially because they're nocturnal!). Although you may be ready to take home hermit crabs, here are some things to consider when deciding whether your home is hermie-friendly:

✔ If your home is constantly noisy, your crabs may not have the peace and quiet they need to rest. This can stress them out and make them antisocial. (Face it; you'd get cranky too if you couldn't get all the sleep you need!)

✔ Air quality and temperature is important for hermies. Do you like to leave the windows open year-round or blast the air conditioner all summer? Do you use a lot of chemicals (cleaning products, hairspray, flea or tick sprays, or spray air fresheners) in the home? Does anyone in the house smoke? If you use any of these products regularly, don't expose your hermit crabs to the fumes. Cover the tank or move it into another room temporarily. Pollutants in the air can irritate your crabs' gills and make them sick.

✔ Do you have other animals in the home? Believe it or not, most people forget about the pets that they already have before they bring another one home. A big dog can knock the crabitat off the table by accident when you aren't home, and cats and ferrets are notoriously curious and something as interesting as a hermit crab may excite their natural hunting instincts.

✔ How devoted are you to the living things you bring home? Will you make caring for your hermit crabs a priority? If you procrastinate when it comes to taking care of your other pets, you may want to reconsider owning hermit crabs. Although their needs are simple, hermies require specific daily care — without it, they will get sick and die.

How Young Is Too Young? Hermit Crabs and Children

If you are buying a hermit crab for a child, be realistic about the crab's care. Although a five-year-old may think that a hermit crab is a neat pet, will he or she remember to change the crab's water each day? Probably not.

If you're the parent of a potential hermit crab owner, there's a good possibility that you may end up being the hermit crab's sole caretaker. Before you let your child get a hermie, consider whether you'll have the time in your daily schedule to care for the crabs if your child doesn't. On the other hand, keeping hermit crabs can be great learning experiences for children and make good pets for classrooms and school-age children (with the proper supervision, of course!).

If your hermit crabs are going to be around children (no matter what age the children are), make sure they understand that the hermit crab isn't a toy. Even if the hermit crab is living in a color-fully painted shell, the child should know that the crab is a living creature with feelings. A child too young to grasp this concept should not be allowed to handle hermit crabs. (To read more about children and handling hermit crabs, turn to Chapter 6.)

Giving Yourself the Third Degree

Before you decide to buy hermit crabs and bring them into your home, ask yourself the following questions. By considering all the requirements, you will know whether hermit crab keeping is right for you.

- Do I have enough space in my home for a hermit crab tank?
- Can I house at least three crabs without overcrowding them?
- Will I keep the tank temperature and humidity at a constant level?
- Will I check the tank and remove any spoiled food daily?
- Will I change the water in the sea sponge each day and provide clean water to the crabs?
- Can I protect my hermies from other pets who may want to "play" with them?
- Will I always supervise children when they handle the hermits?
- Do I have the finances available to take care of the crabs for many years to come?
- If I have to leave town for more than a week, can someone else take care of the crabs for me?
- Will I handle the crabs regularly?
- Do I really want to keep hermit crabs?

Have you answered all these questions with an enthusiastic yes? Great! Does everything you've read in this chapter excite you about keeping hermit crabs? Wonderful! You're on your way to adopting the perfect pet.

If, however, you're unsure about some of the keeping requirements, or you're not 100 percent inspired to own a tank filled with crabs, you should hold off on buying hermits right now. Maybe you need more time to think about it (or maybe you just need to read the rest of this book to help you decide). But whatever your decision, make sure that crab keeping is right for you.

Chapter 3

Buying Healthy Hermit Crabs

*N*ow that you've decided to own hermit crabs, you need to find some to bring home. (If you're still unsure, check out Chapter 2). Although it sounds easy (you just pick a crab out, right? Wrong!), this chapter shows you several things you need to know about finding hermit crabs and choosing a healthy one. Bringing home a new pet is an exciting time, and you want to make sure you get the best (and healthiest) crabs possible.

Making a Hermie Shopping List

You have a lot of factors to consider when choosing hermit crabs, such as how many and what kinds. This section helps you answer these questions so that you can choose the right crabs for you.

Hermits grow by molting, and the larger the crab, the older it is. Other than that, there's no sure way to determine the age of a hermit crab. So you don't worry about deciding what age is best for you. The keeping requirements are the same for older crabs and youngsters, and nobody can be exactly sure of a hermit crab's age.

How many should I buy?

You need to buy at least three hermit crabs when you're starting out (or more, if you have the space and budget for them). Hermit crabs, despite the name, are social creatures and in the wild they roam in packs of 100 or more and live in large colonies. Theses guys need other crabs around to play and talk with.

You can comfortably house three 2-inch crabs in a 10-gallon glass aquarium. If you are buying jumbo crabs, invest in a larger tank (20 gallons is a good size). In general, you need about one and a half gallons of space per 1-inch crab. (To gauge the size of a hermie, measure across the opening of the shell.) Keep in mind that you also have to add extra shells and other accessories to the crabitat, and the crabs need to have space to play and wander.

Which species?

In Chapter 1, I introduce you to the six types or species of land hermit crabs that are sold as pets in the United States and discuss some of their physical differences. But now you're ready to decide which type (or types) you want to bring home. Owning hermit crabs is a lot of fun no matter what kind you have, so it boils down to a matter of personal preference.

If you are a first-time hermit crab owner, you may want to start out with a Caribbean or purple pincher crab. They are the best-known species and are friendly and easy to take care of. They come in all sizes, from smaller than your pinky fingernail all the way up to grapefruit size and larger. Some pet stores only carry the purple pincher hermit crab, so your choice may be made for you.

The other five species (sometimes referred to as *exotics*) also make great pets and, like the friendly purple pincher crab, all have unique personalities. Ecuadorians and *C. rugosus* crabs tend to be a little rambunctious, while Indonesian and strawberry crabs are laid back. *C. cavipes* crabs like to ignore them all and dig! These crabs range in size from the Ecuadorian, which weighs about an ounce, to the Indonesian crab, which can grow to be the size of a football.

Other than the fact that they all must have access to saltwater to live, the keeping requirements for the exotic species are basically the same as for the purple pincher crabs. (I make sure to note any care or behavior exceptions with the Hermie Help icon. So keep an eye out as you read Chapter 5 on hermie care and Chapter 6 on hermie behavior. You may also want to check out a couple of the hermie care Web sites listed at the back of the book if you want more info on the more exotic hermies.)

Although hermit crabs tend to hang around with other crabs of the same species in the wild, they do mix in areas where the various species overlap, such as in the western Pacific. So if you like variety, you can keep crabs of different species in the same crabitat without a problem. It's a good idea, however, when first introducing a new species to the tank, to watch how it interacts with its tankmates. Some hermit crabs are naturally more "crabby" (regardless of the species) and try to steal shells, guard the food dish, or otherwise cause trouble.

What size?

Choosing the appropriate-sized crabs for your new little crab colony is important, even more important than the crab species you decide to keep. The size of the crabs you purchase depends on a few factors:

- ✔ How many crabs you want to keep
- ✔ The size of the tank you have
- ✔ How much you want to spend on shells and food
- ✔ The size of crabs you already own (if you own any)

It's pretty simple to figure out that smaller hermit crabs take up less space than larger crabs. Say you have your heart set on keeping just three hermit crabs. You can easily house them in a 10-gallon tank and they will have enough space to play and roam around. But if you try to cram three huge, baseball-sized crabs in the tank, they will feel overcrowded and start to squabble. If you want to keep jumbo-sized crabs, start with a 20-gallon tank so that everyone has enough room to roam. (See the section "How many should I buy?" earlier in the chapter for a general rule on how much tank space you need for each crab.)

Smaller crabs are good for first-time crab keepers and children. They are easy to handle and eat less than the larger crabs do. Although small crabs need more spare shells to switch into because they molt more often (see Chapter 5 for more on molting), the shells aren't very expensive. The larger crabs gobble up more food, and the bigger shells they require can cost between 5 to 15 dollars (or more) compared to a dollar or two for smaller shells.

Regardless of whether you want small or large crabs, a good general rule is to choose hermit crabs of varying sizes (see Figure 3-1). Crabs of the same size wear shells of the same size and tend to have shell fights more often, which can seriously injure your crabs. If you want to keep all your crabs on the smaller end of the scale for cost or space reasons, you don't have to get a jumbo crab just to vary things up! Just make sure the small crabs you choose aren't all identical in size.

Photo credit: IHaveCrabs.com/Andrew Lewis

Figure 3-1: Hermies of different sizes get along better.

This rule is also important if you already own a few crabs and want to add another — don't pick a newcomer that's the same size as one of your oldies. However, if you're replacing a crab that has died (which you need to do if you now have fewer than three crabs), buy a new crab that's the same size as the one that died. This prevents bullying from the other crabs. See Chapter 6 for more on bullying crabs and shell fights.

Male or female?

If you're wondering whether you should get male or female crabs or whether it's okay to mix the sexes, stop wondering. Gender as a rule has no effect on the crabs' disposition — males can be as sweet as females — and because land hermit crabs can't breed in captivity (they need access to the ocean), you don't need to worry about them multiplying like hamsters if you mix the sexes. Pet stores don't sex the crabs they're selling and trying to determine it yourself in the store is nearly impossible. Despite the rumors, the size or color of a crab's claw or the amount of hair the hermit crab has on its body doesn't indicate gender. The only way to tell the sex of a hermit crab is to look at its back walking legs. But to do so, you have to wait for it to come out of his (or her) shell. A crab that has been poked at in the pet store isn't going to want to come out on his own, and you should never try to force a hermie from its shell or you could kill it. Both genders make good pets, so sex doesn't matter when you pick out your crabs. However, if you're still curious after you get your hermies settled in their new home, you can go to `www.hermit-crabs.com/sexing.html` for instructions on how to safely determine your hermit's sex.

Finding a Place to Buy a Hermie

So you want to buy hermit crabs, but where do you shop for these little guys? You can find hermit crabs in several places: national pet stores, smaller mom and pop pet shops, gift shops, mall kiosks, and even adoption agencies. With so many options, you may think that one place is just as good as another, but that's not always the case. Table 3-1 lists the advantages and disadvantages of each type of establishment.

Table 3-1	Different Places to Buy Hermit Crabs	
Type of establishment	**Advantages**	**Disadvantages**
National pet chain	Large selection of products; health guarantee; reasonable prices on crabs	Crabs may improperly kept; staff may not be able to answer specific care questions
Mom and pop or smaller pet store	Health guarantee; should have some hermit crab products available	Crabs may be improperly kept; staff may not be able to answer specific care questions; prices may be inflated; may not have wide variety of hermie products
Gift shops	Crabs are usually cheap	Crabs may be improperly kept; no health guarantee; staff not trained to answer questions; may not sell hermit crab supplies; store could go out of business overnight
Mall kiosk	Convenient	Crabs are expensive; crabs may be improperly kept; no health guarantee; staff not trained to answer questions; may not sell hermit crab supplies; store could go out of business overnight

(continued)

Table 3-1	Different Places to Buy Hermit Crabs	
Type of establishment	*Advantages*	*Disadvantages*
Adoption	Crabs usually come with supplies; can meet with previous owner (in some cases); crabs have been taken care of by trained staff	Not sure how crabs were cared for in the past; no health guarantee or refund

Cruising the national pet stores

Large pet store chains, such as Petco, are usually the first place to look for hermit crabs, although you may want to call ahead to make sure they have hermit crabs available. Check your phone book or go online to find a store near you. (The Web site for Petco is www.petco.com.)

Most pet stores offer a guarantee that their hermit crabs are healthy and in good condition. If some problem arises with your hermits (should they die within 24 hours, for example), you can take the crabs back for a refund. Be sure to ask about health guarantees when you purchase your crabs.

Nationwide pet stores usually have employees who can help you find what you need quickly and can recommend the products you need to set up your crabitat and start your new hobby. However, they are not always trained in hermit crab care, so refer to a crab care book, such as this one, or to a Web site set up by experienced hermit crab owners when you're first setting up. (Check out the list of Web sites at the back of the book.)

If you are looking for exotic hermit crabs, a national chain may be your best bet. Smaller pet shops usually only carry the more common purple pincher hermit crab.

National chains also offer you a vast supply of products so you can outfit your entire crabitat in one shopping trip. They generally carry different types and brands of bedding, equipment, and hermit crab accessories in several price ranges so that you can stay within your budget.

Stopping by small pet shops

The second-best place to find hermit crabs (and the necessary accessories and equipment) is a small mom and pop pet store. Smaller pet stores often have someone on staff who can answer basic questions about hermit crabs. However, the store may not offer as vast a product selection as the national chains, and their prices may be slightly higher. Keep in mind that these stores may only carry the common purple pincher crabs.

Checking out gift shops

If you've ever visited the beach and taken a stroll along the board-walk, you've probably noticed small gift shops offering hermit crabs for sale. Or maybe you've seen some at a kiosk in a mall. The crabs are displayed in brightly painted shells and look like toys. Children are entranced by these little guys (who wouldn't be?), and parents may think it "couldn't hurt" to take one home as a souvenir. The entire setup is designed to appeal to a child and rely on impulse buys from people.

But although these crabs may be very cheap, the disadvantages greatly outweigh the low price. Quite often, these crabs aren't properly cared for and may be sick or dying. If the crabs have been housed outside in wire cages or in tanks at the front of the store, open to cold, rain, and direct sunlight, the hermits haven't been kept at the temperature and humidity levels they need. Crabs in these places are often crowded and frequently are infested with mites.

The salesperson at the gift store usually has no idea how to take care of hermit crabs and may view them as mere merchandise, like the flips-flops in aisle five. In most cases, the gift shop doesn't sell the necessary housing equipment or food for the little hermits, and the care sheets they hand out rarely cover the most basic needs of the hermit crabs.

Many gift shops or kiosks also don't offer any type of health guaran-tee or refunds on their hermit crabs. So if your crab dies when you get home, you've not only lost your new pet, but you've lost your money.

Hermit crabs are not throwaway or temporary pets and shouldn't be purchased on a whim while at the beach. These living creatures need daily care and have specific needs. Even if the crabs appear to be in good shape and your child really wants one, make your purchase from a reputable pet store.

It's important that you invest your hard-earned money wisely, especially when it comes to purchasing pets. Don't buy your hermit crabs from places that don't take proper care of them. Although it may be hard to leave a helpless creature behind, rewarding the bad practice only encourages the cycle to repeat.

Adopting your new hermies

Adopting hermit crabs is another option, although not one commonly considered. Sometimes hermit crab owners for one reason or another no longer want to (or can't) keep their pets. (These unwanted hermits may very well be the result of impulse buys at beach gift shops!)

A benefit to adopting a horde of unwanted hermits is that you can usually get them (and in most cases the tank and other supplies as well) at a reduced rate or even free. In some cases, you can talk to (or meet) the previous owner and get some first-hand information about the crabs, such as their personalities and what foods they like.

Be aware, however, that by adopting someone else's hermit crabs, you may be inheriting someone else's problems. The previous owner may not have cared for the crabs properly, and the hermits can be sick or infested with mites. Always examine a hermit crab for signs of illness or other health problems before you bring it home. Introducing a sick hermit crab into your tank of healthy hermits can cause problems for everyone. (Check out the section, "Bringing Hermie Home" for instructions on how to introduce a new crab to your crabitat.) You can look for crabs up for adoption in your area in several places:

- **Petfinder.com:** A national organization that specializes in placing animals for adoption. Hermit crabs are listed under Reptiles and Small and Fuzzy Creatures. All the specific details on how to adopt a pet are on the Web site.

- **Local animal shelters:** Believe it or not, some people bring unwanted hermit crabs to their local animal shelter.

- **Classified ads:** Check under "Pets for Adoption" in the classified section of the newspaper. Many times, the weary owner will also sell or give you the tank and other accessories.

- **Bulletin boards:** Some pet stores (and grocery stores) provide bulletin boards where customers can post announcements for merchandise and pets for sale.

- **Hermit crab Web sites:** Some hermit crab sites, such as www.hermitcrabassociation.com, have an adoption forum where you can adopt hermies and get lots of information from experienced crab owners.

Looking for Healthy Hermits

Regardless of where you go to buy your new pet, you need to know what to look for. This section shows you how to choose and buy healthy hermit crabs, from the moment you walk through the front door to the time when you take your new hermie friends home with you.

Observing keeping conditions

The best place to find a healthy hermit crab is in a store that is taking good care of the crabs, regardless of whether the establishment is a national pet chain, a mom and pop pet shop, or an animal shelter.

When you start shopping for crabs, go with a critical eye. Keep this list of things in mind as you walk around the store and inspect the crabs:

- ✔ Look at the other animals the store is selling. How do they appear to you? (Fish floating in a murky tank is a sure sign that something is wrong.) All the animals for sale should appear healthy and be in clean tanks.

- ✔ Hermit crabs need basic care — a warm and humid tank and access to water at all times. Hermits kept under a heat lamp, in a tank that holds in no humidity, or in a wire cage next to a drafty door or under an air conditioner could be sick (or at the very least not in prime health).

- ✔ The crabitat should have places for the crabs to climb and play, hideboxes, a tidy substrate, and clean food and water dishes.

- ✔ Hermit crabs shouldn't be kept in a tank with lizards, turtles, or frogs or housed in a tank with inches of standing water.

- ✔ Each hermie should have ample space to move about the crabitat and have a place to hideout. If you see dozens of crabs crammed into a tiny tank with no refuge or room to move, keep shopping.

- ✔ Make sure the bedding and food (and water) dishes in the hermit crab's tank are clean. Do you see bits of moldy food in the corners of the tank? Does the tank smell bad? Do the crabs have water and not just a sponge? Is the water murky?

- ✔ Are there insects (such as flies) or other pests living in the tank? If you see flies or *mites* (tiny white bugs) in the tank or mold spots on the crabs — leave.

✔ What type of bedding is being used? Hermit crabs shouldn't be housed on kitty litter or wood shavings — if they are, don't buy them.

✔ If the tank has humidity gauges in it, check to see whether the humidity level is acceptable (over 70 percent).

✔ Check out the hermies in the tank. Are any of the crabs naked? Do you see a lot of crabs missing eyestalks, legs, or claws? All these things are warning signs that the crabs aren't being properly housed.

Go ahead and ask the staff questions about hermit crab care. (The more they know, the better off the crabs are likely to be!) Be suspicious if they don't know the answers to obvious questions or if they won't let you pick up any crabs. Also pay attention to how they handle the crabs. Are they afraid of them or are they tossing them back into the tank? If one of the staff carelessly drops a hermit crab on the floor, walk out. A fall from even a few feet onto a hard floor can kill a hermit crab.

If any pet shop owner or employee offers to completely remove a hermit crab from its shell so you can look at it (or sex it), leave the store! Forcibly pulling a hermit crab from its shell can kill it. Any person experienced with hermit crabs would never attempt this.

 Don't try to rescue crabs from a second-rate store because you feel sorry for them. Doing so only encourages the storeowner to keep selling mistreated crabs — after all, he just made a sale! And very few sick crabs recover from the stress of improper care.

Reporting deplorable keeping conditions

Don't be afraid to walk out of a store that isn't taking care of the animals for sale. (This goes for anything living in the store, not just hermit crabs.) And don't be afraid to tell management why you're leaving. If they know that they're losing business (your money) because of the way they treat the animals, they may clean up their act.

If you feel it's necessary, you may want to write a letter to the store's headquarters, the American Society for the Prevention of Cruelty to Animals (www.aspca.org), or the local chamber of commerce. Tell them what you've seen in the store. This may wake up the storekeeper and force the shop to improve the living conditions of the animals. If things are really bad, the store could lose its license to sell livestock.

You can also make a report of what you've seen at the Hermit Crab Association's Web site (www.hermitcrabassociation.com). An HCA member will follow-up with the pet store and attempt to correct the problem.

Choosing a healthy hermie

The best way to start off your hermit crab hobby on the right foot is to have healthy crabs. But what do you look for? How can you be sure you're getting a crab in good health?

Choosing a healthy crab requires some work on your part because you must take several things into consideration. Here's a quick checklist of what to look for when choosing a hermit crab. I explain each a little more after the list.

A healthy crab should

- Be active and move around the tank
- Have all its appendages (legs, claws, and eyes)
- Be curious about its surroundings (and you)
- Have a clean shell of the appropriate size

Avoid crabs that

- Have no interest in anything happening around them
- Are missing appendages (especially their claws)
- Show signs of mold or pests (mites or flies) on their shells
- Have a bad (fishy or musty) smell
- Dig their claw into your hand when you hold them
- Have started molting

Although this may seem a bit obvious, the hermit crab you buy should have all of his walking legs, claws, and eyestalks (see Chapter 1 for a rundown on the crab anatomy). Although hermit crabs regrow any lost limbs during a molt (for molting info, see Chapter 5), it's a good idea to start out with a whole crab. Crabs that have all their appendages are more active than ones that are waiting to regrow limbs at the next molt.

Hermits in good health are lively (unless they're napping). Look for crabs that are eating, drinking, climbing, wandering around the tank, and interacting with other crabs. These are all good signs of healthy and well-adjusted hermits. Hermit crabs do not have an odor, so avoid purchasing any crab that has a musty smell to it. This unusual odor means that the crab is overheated and may soon die.

Pick up and handle all the crabs you are thinking about buying. Always pick hermit crabs up by the back of their shells and handle them gently. Rest the crab in the palm of your hand and support his weight so he feels secure (see Figure 3-2). (Chapter 6 has more info on handling hermies.) Even though they may be resting when you visit the pet shop (they're nocturnal and the bright lights of the store make them want to hide), they should come out of their shells and investigate what's going on when you pick them up. If none of the crabs is responsive, ask the pet store staff to lightly mist the tank. A hermit crab that is inactive after being misted is either very crabby, sick, or dead.

Photo credit: © Christa L. M. Wilkin

Figure 3-2: Handle and examine all the hermit crabs closely.

However, if the crab comes out claw first and tries to dig his large claw into the flesh on your palm, don't purchase him. It's normal for a crab to pinch anything in its claw (like if you put a toothpick in it, for example), but a digging, pinching crab is aggressive and may hurt your other hermits. Let pinching crabs lie.

The more crabs you handle, the better idea you get of their different personalities. After you find three or more crabs you think are healthy, take them out of the tank and introduce them to each other. Watch how they interact and see whether they get along. They should not be overly aggressive (bullying other crabs or fighting), but they shouldn't be completely lethargic, either. If they seem compatible, they will probably be good tankmates.

Don't purchase a crab that is molting; the stress of moving to a new environment can kill the crab. (Check out Chapter 5 for a rundown on the signs of molting.) Besides, molting crabs shouldn't be kept in the tank with non-molting crabs. A crab in molt is extremely vulnerable and needs his or her own isolation tank.

You also need to check out the shells of any crabs you are considering. The shell should be the right size for the crab. A shell that's a little big is okay (it gives him a bit of extra room), but a large crab shouldn't be squashed into a tiny shell that he (or she) is much too big for.

Don't purchase a hermit crab just because you think its shell is painted prettily. Some hermit crab distributors sell hermit crabs in brightly decorated shells because the colors or patterns appeal to children. But 80 percent of hermit crabs, given the opportunity and a quality, unpainted substitute, will change out of the painted shell as soon as possible. Painted shells are coated with epoxy, which may be harmful to the crab if the shell isn't cured before the crab moves into it.

Bringing Hermie Home

Now that you've chosen a bunch of healthy hermits, your first responsibility as their new owner is to get them from the pet shop to your house so they can settle in. This section tells you how to make the transition a smooth one.

Creating a temporary travel home

The store where you got your hermit crabs should give you a small cardboard box to transport your new pets in. Line the bottom and sides of the box with paper towels to cushion the crabs and keep them from rolling around and crashing into each other.

While the cardboard box is fine as a cheap, short-term method of getting your crabs home, the crabs will be happier if you can transport them in a travel tank. If you have a small isolation tank or you just bought one (the pet shop should have some for sale), line it with a bit of substrate and place the crabs gently inside. Offer them a treat (such as a bit of apple) to give them a feeling of "home" as they travel to your house.

It's crucial to keep your crabs warm on the way home from the store, especially if it's very cold outside. A blast of cold air can kill your hermits or make them stress out and lose their legs. If you buy your crabs in the colder months, insulate the isolation container (or cardboard box) as you carry it from the store by tucking it under your coat. The heat from your body and your coat will keep the crabs warm until you get them home. Be sure to keep the heat on in the car, too!

Making the car ride stress free

Follow these traveling tips to get your hermies home safe and sound:

- ✔ Don't handle your crabs when you're bringing them home. This is a stressful time for the hermits and they will appreciate some peace and quiet.

- ✔ Keep your hermit crabs in their container (or isolation tank) at all times during the ride home. You don't want them to escape.

- ✔ Be sure the car is warm enough for the hermit crabs without being too hot. Don't place the container near an open window or an air conditioning vent. (You don't want your hermit to get a chill.)

- ✔ Never leave a hermit crab alone in a car for any length of time. Besides the obvious problems of temperature increases/decreases, hermit crabs are born escape artists and you don't want to have to look for a lost hermit crab in your car.

- ✔ Keep the traveling container level at all times. Put it on the floor or hold it securely in your lap. The hermit crabs shouldn't be rolling around inside the box or have box "earthquakes" from constant jostling.

Of course, you want a nice home waiting for your crabs when you get them home. For all the ins and outs of setting up the perfect crabitat, see Chapter 4.

Introducing a new hermie

If you're bringing a new hermit home to join a hermie colony that you've already started, isolate the newly arrived hermit crabs for two weeks in an isolation tank. You want to make sure he doesn't have any diseases or pests that can infect your other hermies. The new hermie may also need a little rest after the ordeal of the move before he's ready to face his new tankmates. If he appears to be healthy after the two weeks is up, he can join your crabitat.

The original crabs may be slightly territorial when the newcomer arrives, however. To help eliminate aggressiveness, bathe all your crabs together in the same bathwater so they all smell the same to each other. Also, offering the crabs a variety of shells and lots of food so they all feel at ease helps alleviate transitional stress. In time, they will get to know each other and become friends.

Chapter 4

Creating a Comfy Crabitat

In This Chapter

▶ Creating a home for your hermit crabs

▶ Keeping the crabitat clean

*W*elcome home, hermies! Now that your new hermit crabs are home, you need to give them a perfect place to live. *Crabitats*, as hermit crab tanks are called, are easy to set up and maintain, and this chapter shows you how to do it.

Purchase everything you need for the crabitat and set up the tank before you bring your crabs home. You want to move them right in and not make them wait in a drafty box while you put everything together or rush out to get a few last minute items.

Setting Up the Crabitat

The crabitat is home to your hermit crabs for the rest of their lives, and it's your job to see that the tank is always comfortable and cozy for your crabs. Investing some time and money to set up a good home right from the start makes your new hobby fun for both you and your hermies.

The following list details the items you need to create your hermit's crabitat. (Figure 4-1 shows a basic crabitat setup.) I discuss everything in great detail throughout the chapter, but this list gets you started:

✔ **A tank with a secure lid:** A 10-gallon glass aquarium is best.

✔ **Substrate (bedding):** Sand and coconut fiber are good choices.

✔ **Undertank heater:** To keep the temperature consistent.

✔ **Thermometer:** Necessary to measure the tank temperature.

✔ **Humidity gauge (hygrometer):** To measure relative humidity.

✔ **Sea sponge:** A wet sponge adds humidity to the air.

✔ **Water dishes:** You need one for both salt and fresh water.

✔ **Food bowl:** This should be sturdy and flat (if possible).

✔ **Climbing toys:** Things to explore, such as branches or rocks.

✔ **Hidebox:** Each crab needs a place to call his own and de-stress.

✔ **Snail shells:** Offer at least three extra shells per crab.

✔ **Light bulb:** An optional "moonglow" bulb to see crabs at night.

✔ **Isolation tank/travel tank:** You use the isolation tank primarily to house molting or sick hermit crabs.

Photo credit: IHaveCrabs.com/Andrew Lewis

Figure 4-1: A simple 10-gallon crabitat with hideboxes and climing logs.

Preparing the tank

The best type of housing for your hermit crabs is a sturdy, 10-gallon glass aquarium. (Of course, if you are keeping a large number of crabs, you need to get a bigger one.) The tank must be large enough for the crabs, the food and water dishes, toys, hideboxes, and extra shells. It should also be roomy enough to give the crabs some space to wander. (Flip back to Chapter 2 for a general rule on how much space a crab requires.)

Set the tank up on a solid surface (such as a table, the top of a dresser, or a cabinet) a few feet off the floor. You want to keep curious household pets out of the tank while allowing yourself easy access to your hermits.

You also need a glass lid that snaps or locks securely in place in order to hold moisture in the tank, prevent hermies from escaping, and keep pests and harmful chemicals out of the tank. The lid should also allow you to let air into the crabitat. (Your goal is to keep humidity and moisture in the crabitat but not to let things get swampy.) Look for a lid that has a plastic hinge in the middle so that you can open and close the lid when you need to adjust the amount of air in the tank. All-Glass Aquarium Company makes lids for 5-gallon tanks all the way up to 50-gallon tanks. Look for the lids in the section of your pet store where aquarium hoods are sold.

 You may be able to get a deal on a discounted glass fish tank if you shop around. Some pet stores sell aquarium tanks that leak at a discounted rate. The tank doesn't have to be watertight for your crabs, so why not take advantage of a bargain and cut down on your overall costs?

 Wire cages aren't recommended for crabitats because the mesh doesn't retain enough heat or humidity. Pests such as ants or flies have no trouble getting into the crabitat and can cause a variety of problems for your crabs. Hermit crabs can also get their legs or claws stuck in the wire and injure themselves while trying to get free.

Before you plop your crabs into the tank, wash everything (such as the food and water dishes, sea sponges, and extra shells) in dechlorinated water to remove any residue or chemicals that may harm your hermits. (To dechlorinate water, see Chapter 5.)

Cleaning and reusing sand

If you live near the beach, you can collect sand to use in the hermit crab's tank. It's easy (and cheap), but you have to sanitize the sand before you put it into the crabitat, or you may introduce pests (and other harmful items) to your crabs.

When collecting your own sand, scoop it up from the shoreline. You want dry sand that's as close as possible to the waterline. (You want it to come from the area where the tide comes in.)

After you scoop up the sand, sift through it and take out anything that doesn't belong (like rocks, litter, or seaweed). Take the sand home and spread it out on a clean baking sheet. Place it in the oven at 350 degrees for 30 to 45 minutes. (You're basically cooking the sand to remove the moisture and kill off any pests like sand fleas or mites.) Be sure to stir the sand from time to time so that it bakes evenly. When the sand is done, let it stand and cool for at least two hours before adding it to the hermit crab's tank.

Keeping hermie warm

Your hermies need a crabitat that's between 72 and 78 degrees Fahrenheit at all times. To maintain this temperature, you need an undertank heater. The undertank heater is basically a heat pad that goes under the tank and warms it from the bottom up.

You can find undertank heaters in the reptile section of the pet store (as are most of the hermit crab supplies). Setting up the heater is easy — just stick it on to the bottom of the tank, fix the little rubber feet that are included in the package onto the four corners of the crabitat, and plug it in. You're all set!

Undertank heaters only cover half of an aquarium, so that the crabitat has a cool side and a warm side. If the crabs get too warm, they can move to the cooler section. You can control how warm the "warm side" is by adjusting the level of substrate (bedding) over the heater. (The deeper the substrate, the lower the temperature; the more shallow the substrate, the higher the temperature.) Make sure that the range stays between 72 degrees at the low end and 78 degrees at the high end. You can also put the heater on a timer and have it turn on and off at regular intervals, allowing you to regulate the tank temperature when you're not home.

Don't use an electric blanket or heating pad made for people under your hermit crab's tank. They aren't designed for this purpose and can overheat the crabitat.

The undertank heater is the only heat source your hermit crabs need. *Hot rocks* made for reptiles and heat lamps overheat the crabs and can dry out the crabitat. Also, hermits are nocturnal creatures and don't appreciate a spotlight beaming down on them when they are trying to nap anyway!

Purchase a good thermometer to make sure the temperature stays even inside the tank. Several types of thermometers are sold in pet stores, but the best one to buy is a dial-type that sticks to the glass tank. Place it on the back wall of the tank about 5 to 6 inches above the substrate. Don't be surprised, however, if your hermit crabs find the thermometer and climb around on it. Hermit crabs investigate every item and crevice in the crabitat for escape potential.

Keep the crabitat away from drafty doors, windows, and air conditioning vents to avoid chilling the crabs. Also keep it out of direct sunlight because the crabs can overheat. Keep the crabitat at an even temperature at all times. Consistency is best!

Purple pincher crabs are hardier and can better handle temperature fluctuations than the other species. Ecuadorian and strawberry hermit crabs in particular are very sensitive to dramatic changes in temperature. If you are going to own exotic hermit crabs, make an extra effort to ensure the temperature remains consistent.

Controlling the humidity

Hermit crabs not only need a warm tank, but also one that is humid and moist in order to keep their gills moist, prevent dehydration, and molt safely. (I discuss molting in Chapter 5.)

Keep the relative humidity level in the crabitat at 70 to 80 percent. To monitor the humidity, you need a *hygrometer* or humidity gauge (found in the reptile section of the pet store). The hygrometer looks like a thermometer and attaches to the side of the tank. (Some stores sell combination thermometers and hygrometers in one package.)

Relative humidity is the ratio of the amount of water vapor (moisture) present in the air compared to the amount of moisture possible at the same temperature. *Actual humidity* is the amount of moisture present in the air. The relative humidity in the crabitat should be 70 to 80 percent, while the actual humidity should be in the 50 to 60 percent range. Some hermit crab owners get confused when they see two different ranges, but because most hygrometers just measure relative humidity, you don't have to worry about the actual humidity in the air.

To add moisture to the crabitat, keep at least one natural sea sponge in the tank. A baseball-sized sponge is a good size for a 10-gallon tank. Rinse the sponge in dechlorinated water to make sure it's clean and contains no residue or chemicals before placing it inside the tank. You can either put the sponge directly in the crab's water dish or in a small bowl or saucer with water. Keep a couple sponges on hand, so that you can switch them out on a regular basis to prevent any mold or bacterial growth.

Check the humidity level each day and make sure it's within the acceptable range. If you notice any water droplets (condensation) forming inside the crabitat, then things are way too humid in the tank, and mold and fungus may start growing. Open the lid to dry things out a little. If your crabitat isn't humid enough, make sure the temperature is within the correct range and add water to the dish containing the sea sponge to bring up the humidity. Remember, the warmer the air in the tank is, the more water vapor (humidity) it can hold.

Choosing a substrate

The first thing you add to your tank is the *substrate* or bedding. The substrate should be at least 3 inches deep so that the crabs can burrow under it to get some privacy and sleep. A general rule is to keep the substrate twice as deep as the largest crab is high. Most crab keepers allow for 3 to 5 inches of bedding for average-sized crabs, and up to 10 inches for huge crabs. (Exotic crabs like their bedding to be a bit deeper, so if you're keeping exotics, add a little more substrate to their home.)

Good substrate doesn't absorb water (which would make the tank too damp and messy) or provide pests with a place to lay their eggs or hide out in. The best substrate is sand — after all, hermits live near the beach and are used to wandering on the sand every day. You can purchase special sand from a pet store or regular play sand from a hardware store.

Playground sand (which you can get for about $6 per 50-pound bag) makes a great natural substrate. It's cheap and reusable, or you can recycle it into your garden or compost if you don't want to spend time washing and drying the sand. Choose a bag of play sand that is dry and not torn open (or exposed to insects). If the sand is rust-colored, it's probably contaminated. You can also collect your own sand to use in the crab's tank, but you must sanitize it before you put it in the crabitat. One advantage to using natural sand is that it's easy to find — especially if you live near the beach. See the sidebar "Cleaning and reusing sand" to learn how to do this.

If you want to purchase substrate from the pet store, Calci-Sand makes a good one. This substrate is actually powdered calcium carbonate, which the crabs can eat to strengthen their exoskeleton. Calci-Sand doesn't grow mold, pests can't hide in it, and it's reusable. Be aware, however, that Calci-Sand clumps if it gets wet, and your crabs could have a hard time digging into it.

Coconut fiber bedding (also known as *forest bedding*) is another popular substrate with hermit crab keepers because it increases the moisture in the crabitat without becoming moldy. It also doesn't need to be replaced as often because hermit crab feces decompose naturally in this bedding, cutting down on tank maintenance. After you have set up a tank using forest bedding, you need only to mist the bedding if it becomes dry.

Coconut fiber bedding can attract pests like mites, spiders, and fungus gnats, which can be dangerous to your hermies. Keep unwanted guests out of the crabitat by placing no-see-um netting (available at camping-supply stores) over the tank.

 Exotic hermit crabs seem to favor coconut fiber bedding over other substrates because it more closely mimics their natural habitat and allows them to dig easily.

Avoid using the following substrates in your hermit crab's tank:

- ✔ **Wood shavings:** These get damp, absorb too much moisture, and may house pests. Especially avoid any shavings or chips made from pine or cedar. Cedar products give off dangerous chemicals and are hazardous to an animal's health. Do not use them in any animal's home.

- ✔ **Cat litter:** Hermit crabs are not cats! Litter is uncomfortable to your crabs and can be hazardous to their health.

- ✔ **Garden dirt or potting soil:** These may contain fertilizers, pesticides, or pests that can make your crabs sick (or worse!).

- ✔ **Paper towels or recycled newspaper bedding:** These become too wet from the humidity in the tank and don't help retain heat.

- ✔ **Corn cob bedding:** Hermies can't burrow under this bedding and it's also rough on their legs.

- ✔ **Ground walnut or coconut shells:** These beddings are intended for use in a desert-like dry environment. The walnut or coconut shells retain moisture, stick to the hermit crab's exoskeleton, and drains moisture from your hermie.

 Never buy any substrate that has been treated with chemicals or pesticides — this can kill your crabs!

Lighting up the crabitat

Hermit crabs don't require any special lighting, so you don't have to worry about ultraviolet lights, black lights, or heat lamps. You can, however, provide your crabs with a moonglow bulb sold in pet stores. One 15-watt bulb simulates a moonlit night so that you can watch your crabs in the dark when they're most active. Pet stores sell various types of lamp set-ups. Buy one that attaches to outside of the tank so the light shines down on your crabs.

Choosing food and water dishes

Your crabs need three bowls in their tank: one for food, one for salt water, and one for fresh water. All three dishes should be made of a non-porous and non-metallic material. You can get many types of dishes in pet stores, although most crab owners purchase dishes made of sturdy plastic or resin.

Get a food dish that's shallow enough for the crabs to get in and out of easily. You can even get dishes that have steps molded into the plastic (although stairs are more important for the water bowls). Choose a bowl in the size and shape that best fits the size of the crabitat and the number of crabs you have. (The more crabs you house, the larger the food dish you need.) Crabs of all sizes can share the same food bowl, but if you suspect that your tiny crabs are being bullied by larger crabs and not getting enough to eat, add another dish to the tank.

Hermies use the water bowls to bathe themselves, replenish the reserve supply of water in their shells, and take a drink. Make sure the bowl is wide enough for your largest crab to sit his entire body (shell and all) in and is about a quarter-inch to a half-inch deep. If it's any deeper, the hermit crabs can drown because their gills are down by their legs. If you use a seashell as a water dish, be sure that the water in the back of the dish isn't so deep that your smaller crabs will drown. If in doubt, put a sponge in the dish. The crabs can use the sponge to climb out of the dish if they need to.

Don't use regular tap water in the crabitat. Purchase a bottle of chemical dechlorinator at the pet store. Check out the aquarium-product aisle for an assortment of tap water conditioners you can use to make your water hermit-crab friendly. (See Chapter 5 for more on water treatment.)

Exotic crabs must have access to saltwater at all times in order to survive. Offer your purple pincher crabs a dish of salt water as well because they would have access to it in the wild.

Accessorizing your crabitat

So what else should you put in the tank besides the substrate, the feeding dishes, and the crabs? Plenty! Hermit crabs like to be busy and love exploring their surroundings, so provide them with a variety of toys, extra shells, things to climb, and hermit hideouts.

You can decorate the crabitat with artificial plants, vines, and other accessories found in the aquarium aisle or reptile section of your pet store. Feel free to rearrange the furnishings and toys in the crabitat from time to time. The hermits appreciate the change of scenery and finding new places (and things) to explore keeps them from getting bored.

Although you can add live plants to the crabitat, odds are that the crabs are going to dig them up, eat them, or otherwise destroy them, so it may not be worth your effort. If you do put live plants in the tank, make sure they were grown under organic conditions and aren't poisonous to hermit crabs.

Playing with toys and shells

All hermit crabs need exercise. In the wild, they roam for a mile or more each night. Although you can't let your crabs out to wander around the neighborhood, you can keep them busy and active with toys and exercise areas. Crabs like to climb, so add some ladders, hammocks, branches, or ramps to the tank. Some hermie owners use household items (like plate stackers, overturned baskets, and plastic canvas) to make different levels for the crabs to play on and explore. Use your imagination and create new climbing "jungle gyms" for your crabs.

You can give the crabs real branches and stones or plastic ones (the crabs don't care whether their toys are real or made of resin). If you do bring driftwood, coral, or other natural items into the tank, make sure they aren't a resinous wood such as pine or cedar. Microwave all natural items for a few minutes to kill any mold or bugs. (Two to three minutes in the microwave sterilizes the accessories thoroughly. Be sure to let them cool off before you return them to the crabitat.)

Make sure that the crabs can't get trapped (or get their claws or legs stuck) in any toys you add to the crabitat. Don't put any painted ceramic items in the tank — any chips can harm your crabs.

Hermit crabs are constantly on the lookout for a newer, better (or at least different) shell and are happiest if they have a number to choose from. (Hermies that can't switch shells get very crabby.) Keep at least three shells per crab in the tank at all times so your hermies can house-swap when they feel the need.

You can collect shells in the wild, order them online, or buy them at your local pet store. Before you add any new shells to your crabitat, boil them for five minutes and rinse with dechlorinated water to remove any residue, dirt, or chemicals that may be on them.

Hide and go seek: Hermit hideouts

Hermit crabs need a place to hide out and nap during the day or to get away from their tankmates and de-stress. Try to provide a hermit hideout (also known as a hidebox or cave) for each crab. If you don't have enough room for one hidebox per crab, at least provide places where smaller crabs can get away from large crabs if they want to.

Plastic or resin hideboxes come in a variety of shapes, styles, and sizes — some look like little rock caves. You can also make your own out of an unpainted terra cotta flowerpot. Bury the flowerpot on its side halfway into the substrate. The crab will investigate it and move right in.

Going to the cabin: An isolation tank

Your hermies need a second home to chill out in whenever they're sick or molting. This second home is called an *isolation tank* (or an iso tank or hospital tank). A 5-gallon glass tank works well because the iso tank only houses one crab at a time and so doesn't need to be as large as the main crabitat. Your sick and molting hermies still need a warm, humid atmosphere, however, so outfit the iso with all the regular tank necessities: substrate, thermometer, humidity gauge, undertank heater, and food and water dishes. You probably won't need to provide any toys, though.

Note that molting hermies have to bury themselves deeply, so your iso tank needs at least 6 inches of substrate. For more on preparing the tank for molting crabs, see Chapter 5.

Plastic critter keeper tanks can be used iso tanks in a pinch. If you use a plastic container, be sure that the bottom is thick enough to withstand the heat from the undertank heater. Cover the vents in the lid with plastic wrap to retain humidity in the tank.

Iso tanks also come in handy in the following situations:

- Transporting the crabs from one place to another (a plastic tank is a good choice for a traveling container because it is much lighter than a glass tank).

- Cleaning out the crabitat (the iso tank gives the hermies a safe place to play while you clean).

- Quarantining a new crab to check for parasites before you introduce him to your healthy hermie colony (see Chapter 3 for more on quarantining new hermies).

Hermie Housekeeping

Crabitat maintenance is easy, but a daily responsibility. The good news is that hermit crabs don't make stinky messes, although they have been known to bury food under the substrate and forget about it. Moldy food and stagnant water can cause health problems for your crabs, so take time every day to inspect the tank and tidy up.

 If you're going on vacation and can't take care of your crabs, show a reliable friend or relative how to do it before you leave. Sometimes written instructions aren't clear enough (especially if the person has never kept hermits), and your crabs may suffer if they are improperly tended to.

Daily cleaning (or tidying) of the crabitat requires about 15 minutes of your attention, although allow more time for playing with the cute crabbies that are sure to distract you! Each day you need to:

- ✔ Remove uneaten fresh food from the tank. Fresh food left in the tank can mold or attract pests such as ants and flies.

- ✔ Check the water bowls and refill them with clean water if they need it. If the bowls are full of substrate, rinse them out and wipe them off with paper towels. Don't use soap to clean them!

- ✔ Squeeze out the sea sponge and rinse it (in dechlorinated water) until it smells clean; then place it back in the tank. If additional disinfecting is needed, let the sponge dry completely and then put it in the microwave for two minutes. (If it's moist or damp when you put it in the microwave, it will quickly shrink to the size of a walnut.)

 Although the crabitat must be kept clean, don't use harsh cleaning products such as bleach or ammonia in or around the tank. Hermit crabs are very sensitive to chemicals and they can die if exposed to them.

In addition to the daily chores, each week you should:

- ✔ Wipe down the sides of the tank with a paper towel. This removes any condensation and build-up on the inside of the tank. It also keeps your view of your crabitat nice and clear.

- ✔ Add new shells or switch out the shells in the tank.

  Shake the substrate out of the shells that are in the tank and make sure they are clean.

- ✔ Check to see whether any crabs look like they are preparing to molt (I give you all the signs of molting in Chapter 5). Remove ready-to-molt crabs from the crabitat into the isolation tank.

Once a month, give the entire crabitat a thorough cleaning. This process can take a while, so block out a couple hours to devote to cleaning:

✔ Remove everything from the tank and clean it. This means everything — the substrate, climbing branches, food and water dishes, hideboxes, shells, toys, and so on. (Move the crabs into an isolation tank or let them play in a safe area outside the crabitat.)

If you are using forest bedding as a substrate, you only need to replace it every three months. Just scrape off the top inch or two of the soiled bedding and throw it away. Then turn up the rest of the bedding and mist it (if necessary).

✔ Clean the entire tank with hot water (you can use a mild water and vinegar solution if things are very dirty) and dry it thoroughly with paper towels. (Leave the clean crabitat in the sun to dry if you want.)

✔ Wash and scrub all the toys, ramps, food dishes, and anything else that was in the crabitat. Use a scrub brush on the plastic and resin toys and dishes, sterilize wood items by baking or microwaving them, and boil clean the extra snail shells.

✔ Replace or clean the substrate. If you're reusing sand, sift it to get out any particles of food, feces, or bits of shells that the crabs have left behind, and then bake it for 30 minutes at 350 degrees to sterilize and dry it. (You can also leave the sand out to dry in the sun, but be sure no insects can contaminate it while it's drying.)

Plan ahead and keep a batch of clean sand handy. This way, you can pour the clean sand into the tank when it's time to change the substrate, and your crabs won't be kept waiting while the freshly cleaned sand bakes and cools. Be sure the tank is completely dry before you add the substrate, or you'll have a mess on your hands.

When you're all done, put the crabs back in the tank and watch them explore their clean home!

To save time when cleaning the crabitat, buy a second set of bowls and an extra sea sponge (or two). When you clean the tank, you can simply replace the dirty bowls and sponge with the clean ones right away.

Don't introduce anything new into the crabitat unless you're sure that it's clean, pest-free, and chemical-free. If you find an unusual shell or a nice piece of driftwood you'd like to give to your crabs, clean it (by baking or microwaving) first to eliminate any chance of contamination. Keep the crabitat clean, and your hermits will be happy!

Chapter 5

Caring for Your Hermit Crabs

• •

In This Chapter

▶ Feeding your hermit crabs

▶ Providing the proper water

▶ Bathing and misting your hermits

▶ Understanding the molting process

• •

Although hermit crabs are easy to care for, they do have specific needs. Some of these needs are daily, like providing the right kinds of food and water. Other needs, like bathing and molting care, don't require such frequent attention but are just as important.

Don't worry if you're not sure what hermits eat or if you tremble at the thought of a molting crab — this chapter covers everything you need to know to care for your crabbies.

You can use the following checklist to make sure you have everything on hand that you need to keep your hermit crabs happy and well-cared for every day. Plan ahead and pick up the necessary supplies before you bring your hermits home. All of these important items can be found at your local pet store or ordered online.

- ✔ **Hermit crab food:** To provide necessary nutrients.
- ✔ **Calcium and carotene supplements:** To keep your hermie's exoskeleton healthy.
- ✔ **Salt:** Rock or sea salt or an aquarium salt safe for hermit crabs.
- ✔ **Water dechlorinator:** This removes harmful chemicals, metals, and chlorine from tap water.
- ✔ **Misting bottle:** Used to hydrate the crabs.
- ✔ **Bathing tub:** A small tub to bathe your hermit crabs.
- ✔ **Water conditioner:** To help moisturize the crabs.
- ✔ **Isolation tank:** Necessary to isolate molting crabs.
- ✔ **New snail shells:** Keep a variety of shells in the crabitat.

Dinner Time! Eating Heathy

Here's some good news: Hermit crabs aren't fussy eaters and they don't gobble up a lot of food. Hermit crabs are *omnivores*, which means they eat both plant and animal matter. In their natural habitats, they are experienced scavengers and roam the beaches and surrounding areas in search of food. They like a variety of foods in their diets and eat anything that they find interesting, such as wood, grass, leaf litter, nuts, bits of dead fish, insects, flowers, and fruits and vegetables.

In captivity, hermies eat many of the same foods that you do, so you can shop for your hermit's dinner while you shop for your own (this is always a plus). Of course, hermies still have their own special dietary needs, but by feeding them a combination of commercially prepared food, fresh fruits, vegetables, and meat, they have exactly what they need to stay healthy. This section runs down good hermie foods, as well as how often and how much these little critters eat.

Buying commercial foods

The best way to be sure your crabs are getting a balanced diet is to give them commercially prepared hermit crab food in addition to snacks and treats of fresh fruits and vegetables.

A store-bought brand of hermit crab food provides vitamins, minerals, and protein the hermits need to stay healthy. Check the label for a brand that's low in preservatives and contains carotene and calcium, which are very important to hermie health. However, you can also give crabs calcium and carotene supplements, so the hermit food doesn't have to provide them. (See the section "Take Your Vitamins, Little Hermie" for more on supplements.)

You can find a variety of types and brands in the hermit crab section of your pet store. The most common hermit crab food is a pelleted form. However, very small hermit crabs and sick hermies can't get their pinchers around a pellet and may suffer from malnutrition as a result. Always grind up any pelleted food for your hermit crabs. If you don't want to mess with grinding pellets, look for hermie food that's sold in flakes, cakes, or meals.

Avoid crab foods that smell bad to you — hermit crabs have an excellent sense of smell and avoid those foods. (The exception to this rule is any kind of dried shrimp, krill, or sea life. They reek, but hermies need them on a semi-regular basis in order to get enough carotene in their diet). If you're unable to sniff before you buy and don't have another option, you can punch stinky food up a bit by adding regular, non-instant oatmeal, dried fruit (without sulfites), or plain, unseasoned bread crumbs.

 If your local pet store doesn't carry commercially prepared hermit crab food, you can order it online from hermit crab supply stores such as www.petdiscounters.com or www.thehermiehut.com. Florida Marine Research (FMR) crab food and treats are widely regarded as some of the best crab food available. FMR is a wholesale-only company, but you can purchase their products at many stores and at the two Web sites I just mentioned.

Feasting on fresh foods

Hermit crabs eat a variety of fruits, vegetables, and meats. Rinse fresh fruits and vegetables in dechlorinated water and cut them in small pieces before you place them in the food dish (see the section "Water: The Key to Good Hermie Health" for info on dechlorinating water). This washes off any pesticides, dirt, or chemicals that can make your crabs ill.

Hermies like to eat anything found in the produce aisle, including:

- Apples
- Bananas
- Blueberries
- Broccoli
- Carrots
- Celery
- Coconuts
- Grapes
- Mangoes
- Melons
- Oranges
- Papayas
- Pears
- Pineapples
- Raisins
- Strawberries
- Romaine lettuce
- Seaweed
- Spinach

In addition to fruits and vegetables, you can offer your crabs some of the following foods:

- Brine shrimp (and freeze-dried shrimp)
- Crackers (unsalted)
- Dry cereal (unsweetened)
- Fish and shellfish (cooked or raw)
- Nuts (unsalted)
- Oatmeal
- Peanut butter
- Plain rice cakes
- Popcorn (unsalted)
- Rice
- Leftover bones (wash off any seasoning first)

Although hermit crabs aren't finicky eaters, they like variety in their diets. (Who wants to eat the same boring food every day?) Offer them different foods to see which ones they prefer. Each crab has his own likes and dislikes and will gobble up his favorite first.

Although your hermits may like cookies, hot dogs, and other types of junk food, it's not healthy for their little systems. Offer your crabs healthy treat alternatives, such as bits of turkey, fish food flakes, shrimp tails, applesauce, trail mix, cooked egg, and honey.

Hermit crabs have trouble digesting some foods, including dairy products, starchy foods like potatoes and bread, and highly acidic tomatoes. Iodine is extremely poisonous to hermit crabs, so don't offer them anything covered in iodized salt (like crackers or nuts).

When to feed

Although you may think that hermies like to eat when we do and wake up to a nice breakfast, remember that they're nocturnal. Therefore, the best time to feed your hermit crabs is around dusk (or just before you go to bed). The crabs are up and active at that time and looking for food. In the wild, they hunt for food at dusk and they continue this behavior in their crabitat.

Set up a scheduled feeding time for your crabs. If you feed them at the same time every night, they learn to expect the food and eagerly await your arrival. (In Figure 5-1, hermie is grabbing some bananas from the dish.)

Photo credit: IHaveCrabs.com/Andrew Lewis

Figure 5-1: Hermit crabs like fresh fruits and vegetables.

You can feed the hermits every day or every other day, depending on the number of crabs in the tank and how much they eat. Believe it or not, hermits may not eat every day and can even go for a week (or more) without eating. But you still need to provide food regularly so that they can decide when to eat or not.

Remove any uneaten fresh foods from the crabitat each day (even if you don't feed the crabs every day). If the food is left in the tank, it can spoil and mold, which makes your crabs sick.

How much to feed

Hermit crabs have tiny mouths and even smaller stomachs, so they don't need a lot of food. The amount of food you place in the tank depends on the number of crabs you're keeping and their size.

The best way to find out how much your crabs eat is to monitor them and experiment with the portions of food you put in the food dish. To start off, offer each of your hermits a pinch of prepared crab food (in addition to fruits and vegetables) every day. If they eat all the food overnight, add more food to the bowl the next day. However, if most of the food is leftover, cut back on the portions. Also note what types of food they're eating. (If nobody touches the carrots, you may want to try another vegetable.)

Remember, hermies take food and hide it to eat later, so be sure they're actually eating the food and not just hoarding it. Keep in mind that each hermit is different and has his or her own appetite and food preferences.

Newly purchased crabs often eat large amounts of food. Don't be alarmed — they won't pop. They just weren't fed enough in the pet store.

But what do you do if the food doesn't seem touched — are the crabs starving? Probably not. Because hermies don't need to eat every day, they just may not be hungry. You may also be offering them too much food, and they can't consume all that's available.

Hermit crabs eat very slowly, so you may not have the time (or desire) to sit up all night and watch to see whether they're eating enough. If you're really concerned about your crabs, cut back on the portions offered, take note of the placement of the food in the bowl, and smooth out the substrate around the food. In the morning, you can tell whether crabs have been near the dish and whether the food has been moved around. If so, the crabs are eating, but you just haven't noticed it. If you're still worried about your little friends getting enough to eat, you can try handfeeding your crabs (see the next section), but don't force food on them. If you pick them up to handfeed them and they are more interested in pushing the food away and escaping your hand, they aren't hungry.

Handfeeding your hermies

Handfeeding your hermies is a good way to bond with them while making sure that they're getting enough to eat. Handfeeding is easy, but it takes a great deal of patience. The hermit crab has to feel completely comfortable around you and be used to handling before he will take food from you. (After all, you look like a big scary giant to him.)

Be sure that your hands are clean and free from anything that can harm the crabs (such as hand lotion, perfume, or cleaning chemicals). Talk to your crab in a low, calm voice and move slowly so you don't frighten him.

Take a small piece of food (such as a bit of apple) in one hand, and hold the crab in your other hand. Wave the piece of food in front of the crab's claws. He will most likely take a taste test by touching the food with one of his antennules (the small set of feelers). If the food tastes good to him, he'll take a pinch with his small claw and bring the food up to his mouth. Congratulations!

The crab may take the food into his claw and examine it or break off a bit but then spit it out. This may mean that he isn't hungry or that he doesn't like what you offered him. Offer the crab something else to entice him into eating. If he takes the food from your fingers and then pushes you away, the crab's telling you he can feed himself!

If your crab doesn't eat from your hand the first few times you try, don't give up. The crab may be nervous and not used to you.

Take Your Vitamins, Hermie

A good commercially prepared hermit crab food takes care of most of your hermies' vitamin and mineral needs. However, you do need provide carotene and calcium supplements in their diet to maintain a healthy exoskeleton.

Carotene keeps your hermies' color from looking washed out and is found in most red, orange, or yellow vegetables. You can also provide carotene from dried shrimp and color-enhancing fish flakes. Give your hermies carotene-rich veggies several times a week or add a carotene supplement to the food once a week.

Strawberry and Ecuadorian hermit crabs, in particular, suffer from carotene deficiency. If a strawberry hermit crab isn't fed enough foods with carotene, the next time the crab molts, he will wash out into a pink or even white color. Ecuadorian crabs that don't get enough carotene molt into blue or green. The washed out E-crabs are pretty, but as a pet owner, you are more concerned with their actual health than their appearance.

Calcium is very important to your hermies' growing process. Their exoskeletons are made of calcium and protein (which is called *chitin*), and they lose a lot of calcium when they molt. In the wild, hermits supplement their diets with calcium by nibbling on shells found along the seashore. You can provide your crabs with a source of calcium in one of the following easy ways:

✔ Add a powdered calcium supplement (available in the pet store) to their food. The crabs won't even know it's there, but they'll get all the calcium they need.

✔ Stick a cuttlebone or store-bought crushed oyster shells (both designed for birds) in the crabitat.

✔ Drop crushed eggshells into the food dish. Simply boil the eggshells, remove all the membranes, and let them cool and dry; then crush them up into tiny pieces.

✔ Add a dish of calcium-rich substrate or sprinkle a little bit on top of the regular substrate. Calci-Sand and crushed coral both contain calcium.

Water: The Key to Good Health

Water is the most essential thing hermit crabs (and any pet, for that matter) need to survive. If your crabs don't have enough water (or the right type of water), they will die. Hermit crabs use the water in their dishes for several different purposes:

✔ To breathe. Hermies breathe through gills that must be kept moist at all times.

✔ To replenish the reserve amount of water in their shells.

✔ To drink.

✔ To molt. (See the molting section later in the chapter.)

Keep two water dishes in your crabitat at all times — one for fresh water and one for salt water. Purple pincher crabs don't need salt water to survive, but because they have access to it in the wild, you should provide it to them. All the other types of hermie pets must have access to both fresh and salt water at all times.

Use only dechlorinated water for your hermies' drinking and bathing water — even for washing out their dishes. Most tap water contains metals and chlorine that are harmful to hermits. Chlorine can make their gills swell and blister, which cuts off their supply of oxygen and suffocates the crabs. (A good rule is that the water in the crabitat should be of the same quality you would use in a tropical fish tank.)

Dechlorinating water is easy and doesn't take much time at all. Purchase a bottle of water treatment product designed for use in tropical fish tanks and add the required amount to a gallon of water. Usually, it's a ratio of one drop per half gallon of water, but brands vary widely, so follow the package instructions.

Keep a batch (about a gallon) of dechlorinated water on hand for refilling and washing out the water dishes everyday. This is especially important if you're going away on vacation and leaving your hermits in someone else's hands. (You don't want a friend or relative to give the crabs the wrong water by accident.)

Although using filtered or bottled water in your hermit crab's tank may seem easier or faster — don't. These types of water are more pure than regular tap water, but you can't be sure how much chlorine has been removed. Play it safe and use dechlorinated water only.

To make the salt water for your crabs, simply add a product such as Sea Salt or Instant Ocean aquarium salt to your dechlorinated water. (You can find a supply at your local pet store or order it online.) Follow the directions on the package (generally the ratio is about five tablespoons of salt per gallon of water).

Never add table salt to the crab's water. It contains iodine, which is poisonous to hermit crabs and can kill them.

Don't worry about whether the crabs are getting enough salt or too much salt. The crabs will drink what they want (or need) and create their own balance between the salt water and the fresh water.

Hermit crabs often sit in the water dish to clean out their shells, leaving all sorts of things in the water dish. So make sure you change the water in the crabitat every day. Crabs that don't have access to clean water can become ill. (For a refresher on how to offer water to your crabs, see Chapter 4.)

Keep the crab's water dish shallow enough for them to climb in and out of easily. If the dish is too deep, the crabs may drown.

Rub-A-Dub-Dub: Bathing and Misting Your Hermit Crabs

For you and me, getting wet is just one of the necessary evils of staying clean. But for hermits, getting wet is the whole point: Bathing and misting isn't so much to keep them clean but to hydrate their bodies and keep their gills moist. In nature, they give themselves baths by wandering in puddles of water or taking a dip in the ocean, and they get periodic misting from the great spritzer in the sky (rain). When hermits are kept in captivity, you must continue the bathing and misting ritual to make sure they are well hydrated.

Bathing your hermit crabs

Bathing hermits is easy and a good way to get your crabs used to you. They may be a bit timid at first, but they will soon learn to love bath time (especially if you offer them a treat afterwards.) Bathe your hermit crabs once a week, tops. Bathing them too often strips the exoskeleton of necessary oils and stresses and weakens the crab.

Bathing your hermits can be a pretty active process (the water makes them happy), so gather the following materials together before you start:

- ✔ **A jug of bath water.** Prepare the bath water by adding a few drops of a water conditioner like Stress Coat to lukewarm water (follow the instructions on the package). This product removes chlorine from the water while moisturizing the crabs and repairing damaged skin tissues. (Stress Coat is marketed as a treatment for fish and you can find it in the aquarium aisle in most pet stores.) (No matter how dirty your crabs are, never use any type of soap in the bath!)

  Don't use Stress Coat to dechlorinize the hermit crab's drinking water. This product is for bathing only.

- ✔ **A hermie-sized bathtub.** This can be almost any non-metal container, such as a shallow plastic dish or small bowl. (Remember, the water level will be low, so the bowl doesn't have to be very deep.) Make sure that it's clean and free from any soap residue or chemicals.

✔ **A drying-off area**. Your hermies need a place to run around in after their bath. This can be a large cardboard box (if you have many crabs) or a shoebox (for a few hermies) lined with paper towels. Whatever you use, make sure the hermit crabs can't climb out and escape!

✔ **Some rubber ducks.** Just kidding.

When you're all set, pour about ¼ inch of the tepid Stress Coat-treated water into the bath bowl and add your crabs to the bathwater. You can bathe your crabs two different ways. One way is to put a crab into the water upside down and let it right itself. This cleans out any junk (feces, substrate, or bits of food) that may have gotten into the crab's shell. The other method is to put the crabs in the tub and let them walk around and handle bathing on their own. Either way, the crabs get clean.

Depending on the size of your tub, you can bathe the crabs one at a time or in small groups. Bathing makes hermits more active, so watch them closely. They may try to escape from the tub when you aren't looking.

After the bath is over, take the crabs out, drain the water out of their shells (see Figure 5-2), and let them run around in the drying-off area. Don't put wet crabs back into the crabitat because the substrate will stick to them and get them dirty all over again.

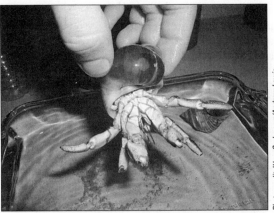

Photo credit: IHaveCrabs.com/Andrew Lewis

Figure 5-2: Drain the water out of hermie's shell after bathing him.

While your crabs are drying off is a good time to give the crabitat its weekly cleaning. Sift through the substrate, make sure any empty shells are clean and inviting, and re-arrange toys and climbing items that have been moved around or knocked over. (See Chapter 4 for more on cleaning the crabitat.) You don't want to return clean crabs to a dirty tank.

Bathe your hermit crabs when you first bring them home from the pet store. A nice bath in lukewarm water treated with Stress Coat helps them rehydrate and alleviates some of the stress of moving. (It also washes off any residue from the pet store.)

Bathing can sometimes bring on a molt, so watch your crabs carefully for molting signs after baths. (I discuss molting in depth later in the chapter.)

It's raining! Misting your crabs

Misting is an easy way to make sure your hermit crabs are hydrated between baths. Simply buy a misting bottle (like a facial mister) and fill it with some dechlorinated water. Take your crabs out of the crabitat for some playtime (make sure they're in a safe location!) and gently spritz them while they're roaming around. Misting the crabs inside the crabitat makes it too damp and encouraging for mold or fungus. The crabs also won't have anywhere to dry off, and the substrate will stick to them and leave a mess.

Misting once a week between baths. You don't want to over-mist and get soggy crabs. If you keep the tank at the recommended humidity level, you may not need to mist your crabs quite that often. However, if the humidity in the tank fluctuates, or you live in a very dry climate (such as the American Southwest), misting your crabs is a good idea.

Growing Pains: Molting Safely

One day you go to the crabitat and pick up your friend to find that a hollow, dead-looking hermie falls out. Don't panic — he's not really dead. He's just molting.

Molting is the process all hermit crabs go through to grow. It's simply the shedding of the old exoskeleton to expose the new, larger one underneath. (Similar to how people lose their "baby" teeth and have new "adult" teeth waiting underneath.) A hermit crab can also regenerate (or regrow) lost limbs and antennae during a molt. A crab that is missing limbs or eyestalks and is about to molt will generate a clear, gel-like substance on the end of the damaged part of the body.

Hermit crabs generally molt once or twice a year, depending on the size of the crab. Smaller crabs that are growing faster can molt several times a year, while larger crabs molt every 12 to 18 months.

Many first-time hermit crab owners panic when a crab goes into a molt, but don't worry. For the most part, you just have to give the crab some privacy and he takes care of the rest. (After all, the crab knows what he's doing.) This section demystifies each step of the molting process and shows you how to care for hermie during it.

Recognizing signs of molting

The hermit that's getting ready to molt usually gives you some clues if you're paying close attention to your crabs. Check your crabs weekly (after a bath is the best time) for any of the following funny behaviors:

- ✔ The crab is digging around the tank, looking for an isolated place to bury himself. In nature, hermits dig into the sand to protect themselves from predators during this vulnerable time. Your hermits will do the same in your crabitat. Figure 5-3 shows a hermie digging in near the water dish.

- ✔ The crab may eat and drink a lot more than usual. This is the crab's way of storing up energy to live off of during the molting process. Hermit crabs store fat and water in a small dark pouch located under their fifth pair of legs. If you see a crab eating and drinking like there's no tomorrow, offer him a few extra treats and get ready for a molt!

- ✔ A just-about-to-molt crab is less active than usual. He may stop moving, seem less interested in playing with his crab friends, his antennae may droop, and his eyes may have a dull, cloudy look. He may hide out and sleep more than he normally does to conserve energy. Some hermit crabs stop moving altogether. Don't panic. The crab is not dying; he's just molting.

Photo credit: IHaveCrabs.com/Andrew Lewis

Figure 5-3: A hermie digging in the sand may be a sign of molting.

Before a molt

If you notice a crab that seems to be pre-molt, bathe him in luke-warm water treated with Stress Coat. The extra moisture and aloe vera helps the molting process along. After the bath, place the molting crab in an isolation tank.

The iso tank should have about 6 inches of sand (or more if your crab is very large) and have the proper temperature and humidity (about 76 degrees and 70 percent relative humidity — see Chapter 4 for info on setting up an isolation tank). You don't have to add any climbing branches or toys to the isolation tank because all hermie's energy will be focused on molting. But he does need a dish of both fresh and salt water in case he wants a drink and some extra shells for him to move into after the molt. Figure 5-4 shows an isolation tank set up for molting crabs. Be sure to keep the isolation tank dark and in a quiet place (like a bedroom or a room that isn't in a high traffic area) — you don't want your crabs to be disturbed during a molt.

Photo credit: © Christa L. M. Wilkin

Figure 5-4: Fill the isolation tank with at least six inches of sand.

Hermie will bury himself in the deep sand of the iso tank, and you may not see him again until the molt is complete. Once in a while, however, hermit crabs don't dig in and molt on top of the substrate. In this case, just leave him be and take extra care that the humidity in the crabitat is kept at the proper level.

But what if you miss the signs of a crab about to molt until he's already started? Maybe you suddenly realized that hermie's dug himself underground, or you find a shed exoskeleton in the tank.

If your molting hermie has already buried himself in the crabitat, you can either set up a divider in the tank to keep him isolated from the other crabs or gently move him into an isolation tank (if you know where he is). You can fashion a divider out of plastic, but make sure it's high enough to keep the other crabs from climbing over it and buried deep enough into the substrate so that the other hermits can't burrow under it to get to the molter. If you don't know where a molting crab has buried himself in the crabitat, it's best to leave him alone. He obviously wants (and needs) privacy at this time. If you try to find him by digging into the substrate at random, you may accidentally harm him or cause him to get stressed out. Leave the crab alone and let nature take its course.

If the molting crab is on top of the substrate, move him to the iso tank to protect him from the other crabs. Gently scoop him and the surrounding substrate out with a spoon and place him in the iso tank. Try to keep the movement as gentle as possible so he doesn't become stressed. If he's already shed the old exo, move it with him; he'll need it after the molt.

Always separate a molting crab from the others in the crabitat. The smell of a molting crab will turn the others into crazy cannibals.

Is my crab dead?

Sadly, not all hermit crabs survive a molt. This is the most stressful and vulnerable time in a crab's life, and crabs that aren't in the best of health may not live through the process.

If your crab has buried himself to molt and hasn't resurfaced in a month, he may have died. If you notice a strong fishy or bad odor coming from the isolation tank, it's time to investigate.

If you know where the crab is buried, carefully move the sand aside and take a peek at the crab. If he's molted and is just resting, gently place something over him, like a large clam shell. Don't try to cover him up with substrate — he could suffocate. But if the crab has died, scoop him out, dispose of the substrate, and clean the tank thoroughly.

Remember that hermit crabs are used to molting on their own in the wild. Aside from giving them a dark, quiet place, there's really nothing else you can do for them at this time.

During a molt

During the molt, your little hermie is breaking out of his exoskeleton by stretching and twisting it until it actually splits and slips off. The old exo (or parts of it) may remain in the shell with the crab or it may fall out (see Figure 5-5). Once free of the old exo, the crab hides out for a while and recuperates (molting is very hard on the crab).

Photo credit: IHaveCrabs.com/Andrew Lewis

Figure 5-5: A molting hermit crab and its shed exoskeleton. (Note the cracked, broken piece.)

The new exoskeleton is very soft and pale, and the crab is vulnerable. He will eat his old exoskeleton to regain lost vitamins, minerals, and other nutrients (see Figure 5-6), while he waits for his new exoskeleton to harden. If the crab's shed exoskeleton gets lost (for whatever reason), give the hermit a cuttlebone, crushed oyster shell, or ground eggshells. He needs all the calcium he can get during and after a molt.

Studies have shown that hermit crabs have two molting-related hormones that enable them to put off molting when the conditions aren't right and to get down to business when they are. (The molting hormone *crustecdysone* helps them along when conditions are right for a molt.)

So what are you supposed to do? Once a day, spritz the isolation tank with dechlorinated water in the general area of the buried crab. (You may not know exactly where the crab has buried himself.) Keep the sand moist, but not sopping wet, otherwise mold could kill the molting crab. (You want to be able to build a sandcastle with it.)

Photo credit: IHaveCrabs.com/Andrew Lewis

Figure 5-6: This hermit crab eats its exoskeleton to regain lost nutrients.

WARNING!

If the crab is on top of the substrate, do not mist him or he may mold. Be sure that the humidity in the tank is at the right level, and the crab has access to both fresh and salt water. If he needs extra moisture, he'll take a drink.

As hard as it may be, resist the urge to peek at the molting crab or check on it. Hermits need a dark, private area at this time. Trust that the crab knows what he's doing and let nature take its course. Never disturb or dig up a molting crab. You could cause his little cave to collapse and suffocate him.

The molting process usually lasts two weeks, but it may take up to a month or more — it all depends on the crab. Larger crabs make take a month or more to molt because they have a thicker exoskeleton to shed and more surface area (the new exoskeleton) that needs to harden.

After a molt

After the molt is complete and his new exoskeleton is still soft, the crab is defenseless and weak. He can't move much or defend himself. The best thing you can do for the hermit is to leave him alone. Let him take care of everything, and he'll resurface when he's ready.

After your hermit has hardened up and resurfaced, make sure that you have a variety of clean snail shells in the iso tank. Your new molter will enjoy trying on the new homes waiting for him on the surface of the iso tank. The new shells should be slightly larger than the shell he just came out of because the crab is bigger now. (I give you the goods on shells later in this chapter.)

When the crab's new exoskeleton has hardened and he is walking around normally, you can put him back into the crabitat with his friends. It may take a few days or two weeks for the exoskeleton to harden completely, depending on the size of the crab. (Smaller crabs harden faster than larger ones.) The freshly molted crab may be more active because he is free of his old, constricting exoskeleton and feels more energetic.

Your hermit crab may actually look smaller after a molt, but don't be fooled. As soon as the exoskeleton swells and hardens, he'll be slightly larger. No two crabs grow at the same rate, though, so don't expect their size increase to be similar.

The dos and don'ts of molting care

Here is a quick checklist of what to do for your hermie when he's molting:

- ✔ Separate the molting crab from the other crabs by placing him in an isolation tank.
- ✔ Provide at least 6 inches of sand as a substrate (more if the crab is very large).
- ✔ Give the crab food, water, larger shells, calcium, and his old exoskeleton.
- ✔ Keep the isolation tank warm, dark, and humid.
- ✔ Change the food and water each day.
- ✔ Give the crab his privacy and leave him alone.
- ✔ Keep other people who don't realize what's going on with the molt from poking in the isolation tank.

Here are the don'ts for when your crab is molting. Tell friends and relatives to obey these rules, as well.

- ✔ Don't peek at the crab, dig it out, or touch it in any way. (The crab will think you are a predator and stress out or die.)
- ✔ Don't throw away the exoskeleton.
- ✔ Don't over-mist the isolation tank
- ✔ Keep the isolation tank away from drafts and excessive heat.
- ✔ Don't move or jostle the isolation tank.

Shopping for Shells

Snail shells are important to hermit crabs because they have no shells of their own to protect their soft abdomen. The borrowed snail shell offers them mobility, protection from predators, and helps the crab stay moist. Because shells are so vital, crabs can be quite picky when it comes to finding a shell to call home. This section takes a look at shell basics.

Why hermit crabs switch shells

Hermits always seem to be on the lookout for a bigger and better shell. Some may only change shells after a molt, but others switch shells like they're going out of style, often going back and forth between the old shell and new shell several times. Here are a few reasons a crab may change shells:

- He likes the shape of the opening on another shell.
- He doesn't like the size of his shell.
- The right twist to the snail shell doesn't fit his abdomen.
- There's a hole in the back part of the shell.
- The crab is just bored and wants a change of scenery.

You may never fully understand the whys of shell switching, but the crabs know what they want, so indulge them in their habit, and you'll have a tankful of happy crabs. (Figure 5-7 shows a hermie switching shells.)

Photo credit: IHaveCrabs.com/Andrew Lewis

Figure 5-7: This hermit crab is switching to a larger shell.

Sometimes hermit crabs take a fancy to a shell that's already occupied by another crab. If the crab doesn't want to give up his home, you may have a shell fight on your hands. This aggressive behavior can injure your crabs, so separate them if you see them fighting. (I discuss aggression in more detail in Chapter 6.)

Make sure you have several shells (at least three) for each crab. This way, when the crabs want to try on a new shell, there will be plenty for everyone.

Providing proper shells

Each crab is different and has different shell needs. The best way to cover all the bases is to give your crabs shells similar in shape to the ones they're already living in (this way you know they like them).

Some crabs like their shells to fit snugly, while others prefer shells that are roomier. If you notice that your hermit can't retreat all the way into his shell and block the opening with his big claw, it's time to get him a new shell. (You should at least offer the crab a new shell, whether he switches into it and stays there is up to him.)

A crab that has molted needs a shell a little bit bigger than the one he previously had. If you're not sure of the size of the shell, you can measure the opening (also called the shell's *aperture*). Large to jumbo crabs need an opening that's about an inch and a half, while smaller crabs need an opening about a half-inch and smaller.

Don't buy shells that are very heavy and expect your tiny crab to lug it around. Check to see that each crab can carry his home comfortably.

The best shell for your crab is the one he (or she) likes. The crab goes by fit, not style, and he will not care what color the shell is or whether it cost you a dollar or ten dollars.

Nearly all species of hermit crabs show a preference for more circular-opening shells and shells lined with mother-of-pearl. The mother-of-pearl feels smoother on the crab's abdomen and provides some insulation.

However, Ecuadorian crabs prefer shells with a wider, flatter, oval opening. (This is because their bodies are flatter and wider in shape). When choosing shells for E-crabs, try to pick ones that look like the shells the crabs are already living in. Buy extra shells at the same time you buy your crabs. Some pet stores may not carry shells suitable for E-crabs and you may have to buy new shells online.

If you collect snail shells from the beach, give them a quick boil and rinse in dechlorinated water before offering to your crabs.

You can order shells online from several companies that sell hermit crab supplies. Most online stores sell shells by aperture size, so be sure to measure the aperture correctly. Call the vendor if you have questions — most places that sell hermit crab products and shells online are happy to help their customers get a perfectly fitting shell. (See the shell retailers in the list of Web sites at the back.)

Basic shell maintenance

A good-fitting shell is important to your crab, but so is a shell that's in good condition. Check your crab's shell at bath time and whenever you handle him. Make sure the shell is intact and doesn't have any chips or holes in it. (A damaged shell can't trap the necessary moisture inside.)

Don't buy damaged shells or give your crabs shells that are broken, chipped, have holes in them, or show spots of mold. These are not good homes for hermits. If you discover a problem with your crab's shell, offer him a new one and hope that he takes the hint and moves. After the hermit moves out, get rid of the damaged shell before another crab moves into it.

Never force a hermit crab to leave his shell to put him into a new one. The crab will not completely exit the shell unless he wants to. He'd sooner be ripped apart than leave the safety of his home.

If you are keeping Ecuadorian crabs, you may notice that they are "homebodies" and don't switch shells as often as their cousins do.

Chapter 6

Getting to Know Your Hermits

● ●

● ●

*I*f a cat purrs and rubs up against you, you know it's happy. If it's arching its back and hissing, well, you've got a not-so-happy kitty. But how does a hermit crab behave? What's normal? What should cause you concern? For a first-time hermie keeper (or even if you've had some for a while), hermit crabs can seem a little mysterious.

In this chapter, I show you normal hermit crab behavior, offer advice on recognizing and dealing with extra crabby hermies, and give you a few tricks of the trade for bonding with your hermits.

Getting in Their Little Heads: Hermie Behavior

Hermit crabs aren't domesticated pets, like cats and dogs, and carry on in captivity pretty much as they do in the wild. Because they live in large groups of a hundred or more in the wild, much of their behavior naturally involves relating to the other crabs.

Gettin' chatty with the hermies

Although this may sound strange, hermits do communicate with each other (and with you, if you're paying attention). They emit a chirping sound called *stridulation* (some people think that it sounds like a croaking frog or a cricket) when they are annoyed, happy, lost, hurt, scared, or when picked up. (You can hear a sound bite of hermies chirping at `http://geocities.com/hermit_crabs/carol`.) Scientists aren't exactly sure how the crabs make this noise.

Don't be alarmed when you first hear this chirping sound coming from your tank of crabs. Crabs click and chirp at one another when they are awake and active. However, if loud chirping and clicking lasts for a long time, check on your crabs because someone is likely annoyed or in pain. A couple hermies may be having a shell fight or stepping on eyestalks, and you may need to referee. Hermit crabs can make quite a racket when they're fighting.

All hermit crabs can chirp, although some do so more often than others. Ecuadorian crabs and *C. rugosus* ("ruggies") are the two most vocal species (which is why ruggies are sometimes called *crying crabs*).

Getting along with others

You may notice a lot of noise coming from the crabitat at night (especially if you're a light sleeper and the tank is in your bedroom). Hermit crabs do most of their wandering, socializing, playing, eating, and vocalizing under the cover of darkness.

When the hermit crabs wake up, they head straight for the food and water dishes, check out what you have to offer, and start snacking if they're hungry. Then, after everyone's eaten, the real fun begins. What better way to pass the evening than to rearrange the tank and have a few friendly wars?

When you check the crabitat in the morning, you may find that the toys have been moved around, the plastic plants are knocked over, the substrate is scattered all over the place, and the dishes have been dug up, flipped over, and filled with sand. Don't worry; this wrecking is harmless hermit crab behavior. Hermies are curious creatures and they can't resist climbing on or digging under anything in the tank. (They probably think it's fun to watch you straighten everything up for them in the morning. And odds are, they're going to wreck it all again as soon as it gets dark.)

Hermies also like to wrestle and climb all over one another. Don't worry; they're not fighting, just playing a game. Let them play and socialize with one another as they would in the wild.

Sometimes two crabs may start a feeler war and duel with their antennae. This behavior is harmless, and the crabs are simply smelling each other. Hermit crabs may also snip and pinch one another on occasion (they're sort of poking one another). However, they're not causing any harm and will let go before any damage is done.

However, if you see one crab viciously attacking another and trying to steal his shell (or if his claws are too close to an eyestalk), separate the two immediately. This is an aggressive behavior display and not regular play (see "Wanna fight? Aggressive hermies" later in the chapter).

Dealing with Problem Behavior

Not all hermit crabs get along well with other crabs. Although they live in colonies in the wild, the hermits have a larger surface area to roam and aren't confined to the close quarters of a tank. This forced cohabitation sometimes leads to behavior problems such as aggression or regression in crabs. If allowed to go unchecked, behavior problems can destroy the crab's happy home and make everyone miserable.

Wanna fight? Aggressive hermies

Hermit crabs aren't naturally aggressive creatures. They tend to mind their own business and live and let live. (Although, like people, they can be in bad moods every so often.) But because of overcrowding, stress, the arrival of a newcomer, or being mishandled, some crabs become holy terrors and can seriously hurt their crabmates.

An aggressive crab may come up to a crab that's peacefully eating and take away his food or hang out around the food or water bowl and prevent his tankmates from taking a drink or having a snack. Occasionally, one crab in a tank of happy hermits becomes territorial when you add a new crab to the crabitat. Always monitor your hermies closely when you add a new crab to make sure the hermits already living in the tank beat up the newcomer.

Shell stealing is a common form of crab aggression. Sometimes the attempted takeover is justified (if the aggressive crab's shell is too small, for example), but sometimes the bully crab just wants what's not his.

How can you recognize shell stealing when it happens in your tank? The aggressive crab (I'll call him Crab 1) knocks into another crab's shell. The innocent victim crab (Crab 2) pulls far back into his shell to secure himself. (Odds are that he was minding his own business and doesn't know Crab 1 has targeted him.)

Crab 1 pounces on Crab 2 and starts shaking Crab 2's shell back and forth. Sometimes Crab 1 tries to put both his claws into the opening of Crab 2's shell and pull him out. If he's under siege, Crab 2 has three options: to fight back; to evacuate; or to retreat and block the shell opening with his claw. Sometimes a "forced trade" happens and Crab 2 leaves his shell and moves into Crab 1's shell.

If you see two crabs squabbling and fighting for snail shells, remove the aggressor from the tank and offer him a shell similar to the one the victim is wearing. It sounds like you're rewarding bad behavior, but you're really just meeting the needs of the aggressor so he doesn't feel he has to steal another crab's shell to be comfortable. It's possible he doesn't know that empty shells are available to him.

If your crabs are very aggressive with one another often, you may have to permanently split them up. The crabitat may be too small for the number or size of crabs you have and they feel overcrowded. Crabs that are stressed from overcrowding can kill each other to get space, food, or shells. They may rip them out of their shells, snip off eyestalks or legs, or attack a vulnerable crab in molt. The smell of a freshly molted exoskeleton can turn a well-behaved hermie into a raging cannibal (they are scavengers, after all). To avoid needless cannibalism, check your crabs regularly for molting signs and isolate them immediately. (For pre-molting signs, flip to Chapter 5.)

If an aggressive crab kills another crab, put the guilty crab in the isolation tank for a day or so and let him calm down. Offer him some food and water (maybe he turned nasty because he was hungry or thirsty). The crab may still be feeling hostile toward the other crabs in the tank and do more harm if he's allowed to wander around freely. After you put him back into the crabitat, keep a close eye on him to make sure he doesn't start picking on another crab. Sometimes the crab's bad mood will pass and he'll settle down. However, if the crab starts more trouble in the crabitat, you may have to permanently remove him from the tank.

Avoid aggressive hermits by not purchasing any that show aggression in the first place. When you put an aggressive crab in your hand, they tend to come out claw first and dig their large claw into your palm. Don't purchase any crab that does this. If you see a hermit bullying other crabs in the tank and causing a ruckus, choose another crab. (See Chapter 3 for more tips on choosing crabs.)

A little aggression from a hermie just home from the pet store is normal, however. He is probably scared and confused by everything happening in his little life. If you bring home an aggressive crab, separate it from the others either by using a divider in the crabitat or by placing the crab in a tank of his own for a little while. Give him plenty of shells, food, water, and tasty treats. Leave him alone if he wants to have solitude, but if he seems friendly, start handling him so he gets to know you and learns that he can trust you.

Where are you? Regressive hermies

Not all behavior problems involve aggressive behavior. A regressive crab that is withdrawn (more so than usual) and isn't acting right can cause just as much worry to a hermit owner.

Regressive crabs may hide in their shells and refuse to come out (see Figure 6-1), stay in a hermie hideout all the time, or bury themselves into the substrate and stay down there for days on end. This "withdrawing from the world" is a good indicator that something is bothering the crab, and the best way he can deal with it is to hide out for a while. A variety of factors can cause regressive behavior and lead to stress, which can sometimes be deadly:

- Being attacked by a larger crab
- Having his shell stolen (that's very traumatic for a hermie!)
- Being prevented from eating or drinking by the tank bully

Sometimes a crab displays regressive signs when he first comes into your home. The move from the pet store and being plopped into a crabitat with crabs he doesn't know may be a bit overwhelming. The crab may bury himself in the substrate to hide from the world.

Photo credit: IHaveCrabs.com/Andrew Lewis

Figure 6-1: Regressive crabs may need a little coaxing.

If you have a shy or regressive crab, do all you can to make him feel welcome. Give him lots of food, water, shells, and treats. (He may not have gotten enough to eat or drink — especially salt water — at his old home.) Keep things quiet around the crabitat until he adjusts to his new surroundings and gets to know his new tankmates. Don't worry if he seems anti-social; he'll come out when he's ready.

Ecuadorian crabs are prone to regression if they are the only one of their species. They slow down, get listless, refuse to eat, and eventually die. Always keep at least three Ecuadorian hermit crabs in your crabitat if you own them at all. *C. cavipes* can be very shy, even after acclimating to the crabitat. Some stay underneath the substrate most of the time and only come up at night to eat and drink.

Bonding with Your Hermits

Who wants a pet that you can't play with? (No offense, fish people.) A lot of the fun of owning hermit crabs is playing with them and getting to know their individual personalities.

The more frequently you handle your crabs, the more social and active they are. Make a point of spending quality time with each crab at least once a day.

The best way to bond with your hermies is with gentle, daily handling. If you're a little unsure how to play with little, pinchered creatures, don't worry. This section shows you how to safely hold them and get them to respond to your voice. I also give you a few tips on letting kids play with hermies.

Holding your hermie

Wash your hands and wrists before you pick up your hermit crab. You don't want to transfer anything harmful to your crab's shell or his body. This is especially true if you've been handling cleaning products, chemicals, or have recently applied perfume, hand cream, or lotion.

Reach slowly into the crabitat to pick up your hermie. (Remember, you look like a giant to the crabs!) Gently grasp him by the back of his shell (see Figure 6-2) so that you're out of reach of the pincher claw and cradle the entire crab in your other hand. Lightly close your fingers around the crab so that he feels secure in your hand. When you pick up the crab, he may pull into his shell slightly, or (if he's used to handling) he may wander around on your hand. If he's a very active crab, be ready to quickly transfer him to another surface, such as a sofa or bed.

Photo credit: IHaveCrabs.com/Andrew Lewis

Figure 6-2: The best way to pick up a hermit crab is by the back of the shell.

Never pick up a crab from the front, put him in your pocket, or close your fist around him. The crab will become alarmed and pinch you.

If your crab pinches you when you pick him up, don't panic. He's not trying to hurt you; he just feels insecure. If the crab thinks he's going to fall, he will latch onto the first thing he finds — you. The only way hermie can hang on to something is with his claws, so don't take his grabbing your skin personally. After he relaxes and realizes that everything's okay, he'll let go.

If a hermit crab latches onto you and won't let go, don't try to shake him off or pull at his claws — this only makes him hold on tighter. Mist his shell with a light spritz of warm water. If that doesn't work, return him to the crabitat. He'll most likely release you after he's back in his home.

When you're settled in with your crab, let him walk on your hand and explore a little. If he's hiding in his shell, he may come out and feel around with his antennae first. (This is his way of checking out the situation.) If all seems well (or you've bribed him with a treat), the crab will come out and walk around.

Hermit crabs that were overhandled or mishandled in pet stores may be reluctant to come out of their shells and may not like to be handled. Be patient and don't try to force them to respond to you. They'll come out of their shells when they're ready.

You have to earn your hermit crab's trust. A crab that feels comfortable around you is friendlier and responds to your touch. Proper handling (and time) builds trust. Always make a point of speaking softly and gently when holding your crab. Avoid making sudden movements because they will seem like earthquakes to the little crab. If you handle your hermit too roughly, he will let you know — with a pinch.

If you are a first-time crab keeper and feel insecure about holding crabs, you can wear thin gloves while handling your hermits. Depending on your experience with hermit crabs and other pets, you may take time to get used to the feel of the hermie's legs and antennae touching you.

Children old enough to understand about hermit crabs and pets in general can learn to hold the hermits safely. Show them how to hold a crab properly and what to do if a crab pinches them. (Keep in mind that larger crabs can pinch hard enough to draw blood.) Make sure that children understand a pinch means "leave me alone right now." Overall, children do better when handling smaller hermit crabs. The crabs fit into their hands easily (making them easier to hold onto and handle). If a small crab pinches a child, the child may be momentarily frightened, but the crab won't do much damage.

Always watch children when they are handling hermit crabs. A curious child may try to pry a hermit out of its shell. Or if a hermit pinches a child, the child may drop the crab. Have the child hold the crab while he or she sitting on a bed, sofa, or on a carpeted floor. This way if the child is suddenly startled by the crab's movement, the crab will only fall a few inches onto a soft surface and not be harmed.

Responding to your voice

In time, your hermit crabs learn to respond to the sound of your voice, as well as to your touch. (After all, you are their source of food, water, and yummy treats!)

You can even train your hermies to come out of their shells (not completely, just enough to walk around and visit) when called. To train a crab to do this, offer the crab a treat (such as a bit of peanut butter or an apple) and speak softly to him. You can call him by his name if you want. The crab will investigate the treat and come out to collect it. If you repeat this often enough, the crab will automatically come out to greet you (and hope to collect a treat for his effort) whenever you call him.

Keep in mind that all hermit crabs are different, and some may not want to come out of their shells on command.

Chapter 7

Keeping Hermie Healthy

. . . .

. . . .

As a hermit crab owner, your primary goal is keeping your hermies happy and healthy. Most of the time, that's easy. Hermit
crabs require very little in the way of medical care. But hermies
aren't without their own set of health issues. This chapter discusses
the most common hermit crab health problems and tells you how
to avoid them. I also let you know what to do if your hermit crab
has an emergency.

Identifying a Healthy Hermit

The best way to tell whether your crab is sick is to know what a
healthy hermit crab looks like and how it behaves. A healthy hermit
is lively, active, and curious about his surroundings, including other
crabs, toys, shells, and the food and water. If he's startled, your
healthy hermie will retract all the way into his shell.

Looks can also tell you a lot about a hermie's health. The following
points describe a healthy hermie:

✔ The shell is clean (aside from bits of substrate stuck to it) and
intact. Any holes or cracks can let moisture escape.

✔ Hermie isn't hanging out of his shell with a dried-out look.

✔ Your hermie's body and shell are free of pests and parasites.
Flies, ants, mites, and other pests can stress your crab and, if
they attack the soft abdomen, kill him.

✔ Healthy hermit crabs don't have a strong odor, so your crab
shouldn't have a strong fishy or unpleasant odor about him.

The best way to make sure that your hermit crab gets a healthy start is to purchase a crab in the best condition. Avoid buying crabs that look ill, are improperly housed, or have flies or other pests living in the tank with them.

Caring for Hermie Health Concerns

By simply taking care of your hermit crabs' basic needs, like providing proper housing, good food, and clean water, you can prevent most (if not all) of the common hermie health ailments. But you always want to be aware of what health problems can come up so that you can combat them quickly.

Many hermit crab Web sites have forums or chatrooms where hermit crab owners can share their concerns, offer advice, and helpful hints on day-to-day crab-keeping. Check out the list of Web sites at the back of the book to find other hermit-lovers to chat with.

You're stressin' me out

You may think that hermit crabs couldn't possibly have stress like we humans do. (Really, what do they have to be stressed about? They don't have mortgages to pay.) But these little guys have a lot on their minds. They're always looking for new shells, keeping their gills wet, and sometimes have to worry about other crabs bothering them. All that can add up to a stressed-out crab, and if the tank conditions aren't right, it can put them over the edge or even kill them.

A stressed-out crab may stop eating, become lethargic, withdraw all the way into his shell, or, in some cases, take out his stress by bullying other crabs in the tank. A crab under a lot of stress may lose limbs and die. Some causes of stress that you need to be aware of include:

- ✔ Constant loud noises around the tank (such as barking dogs or blaring music) that can upset a crab's sensitive antennae
- ✔ Use of insecticides, perfumes, or chemicals around the crabitat
- ✔ Constant or improper handling
- ✔ Being pulled or forced from his snail shell
- ✔ Fluctuating temperature and humidity
- ✔ Too much light in the tank
- ✔ Lack of water or the wrong kind of water
- ✔ Lack of food

✔ Not enough hiding places

✔ Not enough shells of the correct size for each crab

✔ Dirty substrate

✔ Parasites, mites, mold, or fungus in the crabitat

✔ Aggression by other crabs

✔ Over-bathing

✔ Molting (or being disturbed during a molt)

Your job as a hermit crab owner is to watch your hermies closely and to keep the crabitat as stress-free as possible by taking care of the tank. After all, this is the crab's world, and if anything is stressing hermie, the crabitat is the most obvious place to look. (To brush up on how to take care of the tank and your hermies' needs, see Chapters 4 and 5.)

Getting rid of pesky parasites

The crabitat is a good home (and breeding ground) for all kinds of bugs and assorted creepy crawlies because it's warm, humid, has lots of places to hide, and provides the pests with free food and water. What bug could pass all that up?

But mites, flies, fly larva, ants, and other bugs can wreak havoc in a crabitat. The most common pests are dust mites, which are found in every home (yes, yours and mine alike). If you see tiny white or brown rice-shaped creatures crawling around in the crabitat, you've got mites. If left unchecked, the mites can breed and set up a colony inside the crabitat. They get under the crabs' shells and feed off of them and the food you provide every day. A stressed-out crab exposed to mites may lose legs, stop eating, or die.

Sometimes instead of mites, your hermits may have an invasion of another type of pest (usually ants or flies). Flies often lay their eggs on the hermit crabs or in their shells, and when the larvae hatch, they begin eating the hermits' abdomens inside the shell.

Hermit crabs can't reproduce or hatch eggs in the crabitat, so if you're worried that the tiny white things you see crawling around in the crabitat or on the hermits are baby hermit crabs — don't. They're mites or other pests that must be evicted immediately.

If you do have mites or other pests, you need to completely break down the crabitat and give everything a good bake, nuke, or boil. (Except the crabs, of course; they get baths.)

Take the crabs out of the infested crabitat and give them all a bath in lukewarm salt water. Don't use table salt for the water. It contains iodine, which will kill your crabs. Use sea salt or an aquarium salt from the pet store. For the steps to giving safe hermie baths, see Chapter 5.

 Any mites or other pests float on the surface of the bath water, so when you finish bathing the crab, hold onto him and pour the dirty water out of the container before taking the crab out. If you lift the crab out of the water, the mites may reattach themselves to the crab.

Give the crab a quick dip in Stress Coat-treated fresh water. The Stress Coat keeps the crab's internal *salinity* (saltiness) from getting too high and moisturizes him.

Let the crab air dry in a paper towel-lined box while you bathe the next crab. (Do not put the clean crab back in the infested crabitat!) Be sure to change the dirty salt water and Stress Coat-treated water after each crab to be on the safe side.

After you've bathed and dried the crabs, take a close look at them. If you still see crawling parasites, then it's time to go back into the bath water. You'll know that the crabs are completely pest-free when no more mites or pests float to the surface of the water. Depending on how severe the infestation is, your crabs may need three or four baths.

While your crabs are drying and celebrating their pest-free state, take the crabitat completely apart and give everything (all the shells, climbing branches, ramps, toys, hideboxes, dishes) a good scrubbing. Follow this checklist to make sure you sanitize everything effectively:

1. **Throw out the substrate, even if you usually reuse it.**

   It's now infested with mites and eggs, and you don't want to risk reinfecting your crabitat.

2. **Boil the extra snail shells for about five minutes; then rinse them and let them cool.**

3. **Throw out the old sea sponge and replace it with a new one.**

4. **Wash plastic or resin toys and dishes with hot water (don't use soap) and rinse off.**

5. **Microwave any real wood branches or logs tank for at least three minutes or bake them at 300 degrees for a half hour.**

The mites can be deep inside any cracks or crevices in the wood, so don't cheat on the sterilizing process. Watch the wood closely, though, to make sure it doesn't burn.

6. **Wipe the tank down with a vinegar and water solution.**

   Be sure to scrub all the edges of the tank and the corners. (Mites try to hide out in places where you can't reach them.)

7. **Let the tank air dry and add new substrate, tank accessories, and finally, return the clean crabs to their home.**

Now that you've gotten rid of all the pests, take a minute to figure out how they got into the crabitat in the first place so that you can prevent it from happening again. Here are some possibilities:

- ✔ Pests are attracted to food (especially rotting food). Have you been cleaning the crabitat regularly and removing uneaten food each day?

- ✔ Is the substrate attracting pests? The wrong type of bedding can provide parasites with places to hide and breed.

- ✔ Is the tank too humid? Make sure you check the humidity gauge often and keep the tank at 70 percent. (See Chapter 4.)

- ✔ Is the tank lid securely fastened? Make sure that there are no large gaps or openings in the crabitat lid that can let flies or other parasites into the tank. Also, be sure that the lid is kept clean at all times. Spilled food on the lid attracts pests.

- ✔ What's around the crabitat? (Are you leaving food out next to the tank?) Are there any houseplants nearby that could have served as a bridge to the crabitat?

- ✔ Did you recently add a new crab to your crabitat? He may have brought mites from the pet store. Always isolate new crabs for two weeks to make sure they're healthy and pest-free. (See Chapter 3 for more on bringing new crabs home.)

Keep unwanted pests out of the crabitat in the future by placing no-see-um netting (available at camping-supply stores) over the tank. Keep ants out by smearing a thin layer of petroleum jelly around the inside top 2 inches of the crabitat. Make sure that no crab climbing toys come into contact with the petroleum jelly or your crabs could ingest it and get sick. (Only use this method if you have a persistent ant problem.)

Molting crabs are especially vulnerable to attacks by parasites. The invaders will take advantage of the crab's inactivity and eat away at the molting crab. Be extremely careful not to allow any pests to take up residence near a molting crab.

Wiping out mold and fungus

If you notice a musty smell coming from the crabitat, you may have mold or fungus. Mold and fungus build up in tanks that are too humid, have no airflow, or aren't cleaned regularly. They can also attack the crabs themselves.

If you find white or gray fuzzy spots on a crab, bathe him in a solution of salt water, followed by a dip in Stress Coat-treated regular water. Give all the crabs in your tank a bath, just in case they have been exposed to the mold. Make sure they are thoroughly dry before putting them back in the crabitat.

Mold spores can hide anywhere, so you'll have to break down the entire tank and give it a good cleaning. Be sure to wash the tank walls, boil the accessories, and replace the bedding. (See Chapter 4 for a refresher on how to clean the crabitat or follow the instructions from the previous section on dealing with pests.)

Never buy a hermit crab that shows signs of mold or fungus. The infected crab can spread the mold to your other crabs and make them ill.

Mold and fungus are especially damaging to molting crabs. The hermits are soft and weak at this stage and any illness or stress can be life threatening. If mold gets into the substrate with a molting crab, it can eat away at the crab's soft, developing tissues. For this reason, never mist a molting crab directly. Too much moisture can cause mold to grow on the crab's soft exoskeleton and kill him.

Check the humidity and temperature levels in the crabitat daily to make sure it's not getting too humid.

Help! My crab looks dead!

If you visit the crabitat one morning and find what looks like a dead crab in the corner, don't panic. The crab may not really be dead. He could just be molting. (If that's the case, then the crab "corpse" you're looking at is a shed exoskeleton. They are hollow and are often mistaken for dead crabs.) Look around to see whether there is a freshly molted crab somewhere near the exoskeleton. If so, carefully remove the crab and its exoskeleton and place them in the isolation tank. The crab will eat the exoskeleton to regain lost nutrients. (Read Chapter 5 for more on what to do for a molting crab.)

If you can't tell whether your buried crab is dead or molting and don't want to disturb him, wait a few weeks for him to resurface on his own. If the crab is in molt, he will be moving around and looking for food and water by then.

One way to tell whether your crab is dead is to pick it up and see what happens. Although some crabs do die in their shells, most come all the way out of their shells when their time has come. If you pick up a crab that has expired, the body should fall out of the shell and not move. Also check the crab's mouthparts. A crab that has passed on will have his mouth hanging open limply.

Your nose will also let you know if you have a dead crab in your midst. Healthy crabs don't give off an odor, so if you open the lid to the crabitat and smell a strong, fishy odor, it's time to have a crab funeral.

If you find a dead crab in the tank, scoop him out with the sand around him. If you want to reuse the dead crab's shell, give it a quick boil to remove any residue.

If you smell something funny in the tank, but determine that it's not a dead crab or mold, you have to do some investigating. Check the substrate for buried food, shake out the empty snail shells (a crab may have hidden a snack inside one of them), rinse out the sea sponge, and make sure that the water dishes are clean. If the smell persists after you've done all this, take everything out of the tank and clean it thoroughly.

I'm so tired: Hermie lethargy

If one of your hermies seems very lethargic when you observe him, he may just be lazing away the day as he would in the wild. Being nocturnal, a hermit crab tries to sleep as much as he can all day long. However, if you watch the crab at night and see that he is still acting sluggish, there may be another reason for this behavior.

Crabs going into a molt will become inactive. (This is their way of storing up energy for the big event to come.) If your crab is displaying other signs of molting, get the isolation tank ready!

If you know that the crab isn't going to molt, he may be just acting shy (especially if he is new to the tank), or he may be the victim of hermit crab aggression and be too afraid to move around much. Watch the crab closely for a while. If you spot signs of bullying, pests, or molting, you can deal with the situation right away. If one crab is picking on another crab, try to find out why. Is there enough space for each crab in the tank? Does everyone have a place to hide out and de-stress? Try offering your crabs some extra shells and see whether that solves the problem. The aggressive crab may be shopping for a new home. (Check out Chapter 6 for more information on aggression and other problem behaviors.) Your hermits are relying on you to take care of their needs, and sometimes that means you have to guess at what's wrong.

If your crabs start acting lethargic, the temperature may be too low and you need to gradually warm the tank back up to the proper temperature. If the temperature in the crabitat falls below 70 degrees for long periods of time, the crabs will eventually go into a state of hibernation and lose limbs or die. To help ensure that your tank is never too cool, keep the room temperature outside the crabitat above 65 degrees.

My crab isn't eating or drinking

If you think your hermit crab isn't eating or drinking, don't worry. Hermies don't eat much, and you may not be noticing that they're happily munching away while you sleep.

Leave treats out for the crabs or cut back on the portions you are offering. If all the food is gone by morning, you'll know that the crabs ate it. Handfeeding your crabs is another way to make sure they're eating enough. (See Chapter 5 for more details on handfeeding.)

If your hermit crabs look dry, or you're worried that they're not drinking enough water, make sure you're bathing them regularly. This will allay your fears and hydrate the crabs at the same time. If you're bathing them regularly and they still look ashy, they may be preparing to molt. When a crab prepares his new exoskeleton, he draws nutrients from his old exoskeleton to create the new one, making the old exoskeleton look "ashy" or dull.

If your crab is really not eating, he may be sick, or he may just not like what you're offering him. (Either way, you cannot force him to eat, but you can try bribery.) Try giving him a variety of foods to spark his appetite. Or if you know he loves a favorite treat, give him some peanut butter, bits of apple, or fish. Sometimes a crab will go on a "hunger strike" if he's upset or stressed about something. Try to make your crab as comfortable as possible and give him lots of food options. He'll come around when he's hungry.

Handling Hermit Crab Emergencies

Hermit crabs don't have major emergencies, and you never have to rush your hermit to the vet in the middle of the night. However, situations do arise that can be particularly stressful and dangerous to hermit crabs (and very stressful to the worried owner), such as finding naked crabs or broken legs all over the tank. But don't panic. This section shows you how to deal with these two hermit crab emergencies.

How to reclothe a naked crab

Hermit crabs don't voluntarily leave their shells completely unless they are switching shells or are stressed beyond reason. The hermit crab's number one priority in life is to keep his soft backside safe, so a crab has to be literally insane with stress before it will leave its shell. However, they are occasionally evicted from their shells by another crab (see Chapter 6 for the lowdown on aggression and shell fighting).

Even if a crab has been evicted during a shell fight, he will seek out a new shell to live in. But what should you do if you find a crab crawling (or running) around the tank without a shell? (To sneak a peek at a naked crab, check out Figure 7-1.)

Photo credit: IHaveCrabs.com/Andrew Lewis

Figure 7-1: A naked crab may need help getting back in its shell.

The first thing you have to do is catch the crab. (If the crab is upset and frantically darting around, this may be harder than it sounds.) Try to get the crab to run into a plastic cup or something safe that you can transport him in. If the crab isn't moving around much, you may be able to coax him into a container or pick him up.

After you catch the crab (handle him gently!), use the cup method to coax him back into his shell:

1. **Dip the nude crab in dechlorinated water to wash off any substrate.**

2. **Rinse out his old shell.**

3. **Put the crab and his shell in a cup.**

4. **Put a dark cloth over the cup and leave the crab alone.**

   This keeps him from running around frantically and conserves his energy.

You can leave the hermie in the cup overnight as long as you put a little dechlorinated water in the bottom of the cup to keep his abdomen hydrated. If you have a larger crabitat, you can place the cup with the crab inside it so the crab will benefit from the ideal temperature and humidity. If you can't find the crab's old shell or if he isn't interested in it, offer him a shell that is slightly larger than his old shell. He may just want a change of scenery.

Whatever you do, don't force a naked hermit crab into a shell if he doesn't want to go. This will over-stress the already stressed crab, and he could die.

Hermie carnage: Losing body limbs

If you wake up one morning and discover a leg (or claw) lying next to the water bowl, don't freak out. One of your crabs has simply lost (or thrown off intentionally) a leg. Losing a leg, a claw, an eyestalk, or an antenna isn't fatal to the crab.

But why would a hermit crab toss off a leg or claw? The answer is simple — to stay alive. When a hermit crab is attacked or caught by a predator in the wild, the crafty crab decides to let the predator take the leg or claw and drops it. The crab escapes to safety (usually by withdrawing into his shell) while the predator is left holding nothing but a limb. Even though the crab has sacrificed a leg (or other body part), he's still alive and well.

So what should you do when you find a limb in the tank? Not much. The crab that lost the leg is fine and will regrow the missing limb at his next molt.

Hermit crabs can throw a leg at a point in the joint called the breaking plane. (This is known as *autotomy*.) When the leg is snapped off, a cap forms to prevent the crab's limb from bleeding. You can often see a blob of clear gel at the site where the limb was removed (see Figure 7-2). The regenerated leg may not look the same, however. The new leg grows slowly, and it often takes several molts for it to reach its original size and color.

Your hermie most likely threw a leg because he was threatened or attacked by another crab and lost the leg to get away. If you see crabs bullying one another or fighting over shells, separate them and give each crab a few new shells. Although throwing a leg doesn't harm the crab, the constant stress from sudden attacks weakens the hermit.

Crabs that are severely stressed are likely to drop more than one limb. Because almost anything can stress out a hermit, make sure that you are keeping the crabitat clean and at the right temperature and humidity, and that the crabs have access to water. Check for mites and other parasites in the tank, especially if all your crabs are losing legs.

If a crab loses several legs in one day, he may be dying and beyond help. If this happens to your crab, isolate him from the others (who may sense his vulnerability and attack him) and offer him food and water and try to make him as comfortable as possible. If the crab dies, examine the crabitat closely and make sure that none of the other crabs are showing the same symptoms.

Photo credit: © Christa L. M. Wilkin

Figure 7-2: A gel blob forms where a limb was broken off.

A common problem with new crabs is called Post-Purchase Stress (PPS). Within a month of being brought home, it will appear to "fall apart" by losing a lot of limbs at once. A crab with PPS is usually beyond help and the best thing you can do is to make the crab comfortable until it passes away. Crabs with no legs or claws have been successfully hand-fed, made it through a molt, and grew back all their legs and claws, but this is something that only an expert would have experience in.

Keeping Hermie Safe

Although you may think your house is safe, it's filled with things that can be dangerous to a hermit crab. If you let your hermit wander around the house freely (or if he escapes the crabitat) other pets may discover the adventurous hermit and think he's a toy to be batted around the room. Needless to say, hermit crabs don't appreciate this type of "fun" and may strike out and pinch the offending pet.

Follow these tips to keep your crabs safe:

✔ Keep a close eye on your crabs whenever they are out of the cage. They move quickly and could get into trouble before you realize it.

Hermies have been known to wander away from their owner and crawl under heavy appliances (such as stoves and refrigerators), get stuck in heaters, under sinks, or simply vanish into the great unknown, never to be seen again.

✔ Corral the crabs into a safe exercise area or confine them to one room in the house. This way, if they wander off, you know where to look for them.

✔ Keep your other pets away from your hermit crabs. Even though they may just be curious about the hermies, other pets can accidentally hurt them.

✔ Teach everyone who has contact with the crabs how to hold them properly and what to do if a crab pinches them.

✔ Keep your hermit crabs off the carpet if it has been freshly cleaned or treated with chemicals that are dangerous to your crabs.

✔ Always monitor children when they are holding hermit crabs. They may accidentally squeeze or drop the crabs.

Ten Hermit Web Sites

To find out more information on hermit crabs, order supplies, or interact with other hermit crab owners, check out these Web sites:

✔ **www.crabstreetjournal.com**
A monthly E-zine devoted to all things hermie, including hermit crab-related games and activities. See the adoption forum.

✔ **www.geocities.com/hermit_crabs/carol/**
A lifelong hermie owner showcases her two 25-year-old hermies. Good photos of crabs changing shells and molting.

✔ **www.ihavecrabs.com**
Submit photos of your hermies to the gallery or share questions and stories. Also has a great species identification page.

✔ **www.aboutlandhermitcrabs.com**
This site has diagrams of hermit anatomy, species identification, caresheets, classroom lessons, fun facts, a detailed glossary. Send a hermit e-card!

✔ **www.thehermiehut.com**
Stocks everything you need for your hermies, as well as hermie novelties. The products are tested by crab owners.

✔ **www.seashellcity.com**
Order hermies, shells, and crabitat supplies. Sea Shell City is dedicated to their crabs' health: They don't ship crabs during the winter months and express shipping is mandatory.

✔ **www.petdiscounters.com**
One of the best sites for hermit crab supplies. Also buy unusual gifts such as hermit crab magnets and Christmas ornaments.

✔ **www.mrspoppypuff.com**
A great example of one woman's devotion to her crabs. Contains info on identifying the different species and sex.

✔ **www.hermitcrabassociation.com**
Chat with other hermit crab owners, post questions about hermits, share photos, and sell or swap hermie merchandise.

✔ **www.petco.com**
Get a feel for the different types of hermit crab products available and buy everything you need to set up your crabitat.

Nearly Ten Fun Hermie Activities

Make the most of your hermit crab hobby with these fun activities:

- **Got a camera and a great looking hermit crab?**
  Share your photos with other hermit crab owners or enter your hermie in a calendar contest? Check out The Crab Street Journals calendar contest at: www.crabstreet journal.com.

- **Teach your hermit crabs some simple tricks**
  Get your hermies to climb up your arm, perch on your shoulder, or take food from your hand. All it takes is some yummy treats and lots of patience. (See Chapter 6 or www.hermit-crabs.com.)

- **Turn your hermit's home into an exotic paradise**
  Plastic palm trees, coconut huts, and coral transforms a boring tank into a tropical oasis. Add a fake backdrop, red Calci-Sand, plastic rocks, and a moonglow bulb to send hermies to Mars.

- **Enter your fastest hermie in a race**
  Check out www.beacheventsfun.com/Hermit-Crab 2004.htm for a story on official hermit crab racing. Or get a hula hoop and place the crabs in the middle. Lightly mist the crabs to get them going. The first one to exit the circle wins.

- **Go to a hermit crab convention**
  Check under "Convention News" at www.crabstreet journal.com for information on upcoming hermie conventions.

- **Bring your crabs in for a "show and tell" presentation**
  Visit the Kid's Zone at www.crabstreetjournal.com for fun facts, drawing sheets, and puzzles.

- **Start a shell-swapping club with other hermie owners**
  You can sell, buy, or trade shells with other crab owners at www.ihavecrabs.com and www.landhermitcrabs.com.

- **Flaunt your hermie love with hermit crab-themed novelties**
  Buy hermie key chains, T-shirts, coffee mugs, stickers, and magnets at sites like www.hermitcrabassociation.com.

- **Start your own hermit crab Web site**
  Set up a monthly newsletter and display photos of your cool Martian crabitat or your racing hermits.

Index

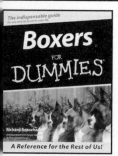

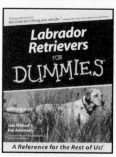
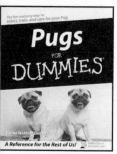
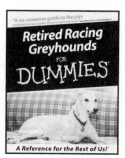

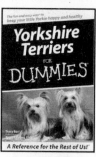
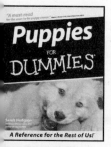

FOR DUMMIES®

Pet care essentials in plain English

CATS & KITTENS

0-7645-5275-9

0-7645-4150-1

BIRDS

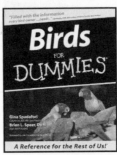

0-7645-5139-6

0-7645-5311-9

AMPHIBIANS & REPTILES

0-7645-2569-7

0-7645-5313-5

0-7645-5260-0

FISH & AQUARIUMS

0-7645-5156-6

0-7645-5340-2

SMALL ANIMALS

0-7645-5259-7

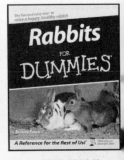

0-7645-0861-X